The Critical Idiom

Founder Editor: JOHN D. JUMP (1969–1976)

16 *Symbolism*

Symbolism / *Charles Chadwick*

Methuen
LONDON and NEW YORK

First published 1971
by Methuen & Co. Ltd,
11 New Fetter Lane, London EC4P 4EE
Reprinted twice
Reprinted 1985

Published in the USA by
Methuen & Co.
in association with Methuen, Inc.
29 West 35th Street, New York, NY 10001

© 1971 Charles Chadwick

Printed in Great Britain
by J. W. Arrowsmith Ltd, Bristol

ISBN 0 416 60910 4

to N O'B

Contents

Founder Editor's Preface

The volumes composing the Critical Idiom deal with a wide variety of key terms in our critical vocabulary. The purpose of the series differs from that served by the standard glossaries of literary terms. Many terms are adequately defined for the needs of students by the brief entries in these glossaries, and such terms do not call for attention in the present series. But there are other terms which cannot be made familiar by means of compact definitions. Students need to grow accustomed to them through simple and straightforward but reasonably full discussions. The main purpose of this series is to provide such discussions.

Many critics have borrowed methods and criteria from currently influential bodies of knowledge or belief that have developed without particular reference to literature. In our own century, some of them have drawn on art-history, psychology, or sociology. Others, strong in a comprehensive faith, have looked at literature and literary criticism from a Marxist or a Christian or some other sharply defined point of view. The result has been the importation into literary criticism of terms from the vocabularies of these sciences and creeds. Discussions of such bodies of knowledge and belief in their bearing upon literature and literary criticism form a natural extension of the initial aim of the Critical Idiom.

Because of their diversity of subject-matter, the studies in the series vary considerably in structure. But all authors have tried to give as full illustrative quotation as possible, to make reference whenever appropriate to more than one literature, and to write in such a way as to guide readers towards the short bibliographies in which they have made suggestions for further reading.

John D. Jump

University of Manchester

I

The theory of Symbolism

Spelt with a small initial letter the word 'symbolism', like the words 'romanticism' and 'classicism', can have an extremely wide meaning. It can be used to describe any mode of expression which, instead of referring to something directly, refers to it indirectly through the medium of something else. Clearly, therefore, the meaning of the word 'symbolism' must be narrowed down if it is to have any significance as a critical term.

A first stage in this process would be to agree that it is not the mere substitution of one object for another – comparing, for example, as Milton does, Satan's defeated legions to 'the autumnal leaves that strew the brooks in Vallombrosa' – but the use of concrete imagery to express abstract ideas and emotions. This still, however, leaves its meaning very wide since, as T. S. Eliot pointed out in an essay on *Hamlet*, the only way of expressing emotion in the form of art is by finding what he calls, not a symbol, but an 'objective correlative', that is 'a set of objects, a situation, a chain of events which shall be the formula of that particular emotion'. Stéphane Mallarmé had said something of the same sort thirty years before in 1891 when he had defined Symbolism as the art of 'evoking an object little by little so as to reveal a mood or, conversely, the art of choosing an object and extracting from it an "état d'âme"' (*Oeuvres Complètes*, p. 869). But he had added that this mood should be extracted 'par une série de déchiffrements' – 'by a series of decipherings' – and in the previous half of his definition it is important to note that he had talked of evoking an object 'little by little'. Both these phrases imply that the 'objective correlative' and its associated mood should not be revealed openly and clearly but should merely be hinted at. This is, in fact, a point which Mallarmé emphasizes elsewhere in the same passage where he contends that 'to name an object is to banish the major part of the enjoyment derived from a poem, since this enjoyment consists in a process of gradual revelation.' The object, he claims, should merely be suggested – '*suggérer*, voilà le rêve' – and he concludes that it is the perfect practice of this mysterious process which constitues Symbolism – 'c'est le parfait usage de ce mystère qui constitue le symbole.'

Mallarmé's disciple, Henri de Régnier, made much the same point when he defined the term 'symbol' as being a comparison between the abstract and the concrete with one of the terms of the comparison being merely suggested – 'une comparaison de l'abstrait au concret dont un des termes reste sous-entendu.' And, as Régnier further pointed out, because the symbol thus frequently stands alone, with the reader being given little or no indication as to what is being symbolized, Symbolist poetry inevitably has a certain built-in obscurity. Mallarmé is reputed to have said that he had banished the words 'as' and 'like' from his vocabulary, and although some of his earlier poems are clearly divided into an opening image followed by a section interpreting the image, in his later poems, as we shall see, he tends more and more to omit, or at least to play down the interpretation and to leave the symbol virtually unexplained. Similarly, the sad and mournful landscapes of Mallarmé's contemporary, Paul Verlaine, are intended to convey to the reader the poet's profound melancholy though his poems rarely state explicitly that this is their purpose.

Symbolism can therefore be defined as the art of expressing ideas and emotions not by describing them directly, nor by defining them through overt comparisons with concrete images, but by suggesting what these ideas and emotions are, by re-creating them in the mind of the reader through the use of unexplained symbols.

This, however, is only one aspect of Symbolism, what may be called the personal aspect that remains on the human plane. There is a second aspect, sometimes described as 'transcendental Symbolism', in which concrete images are used as symbols, not of particular thoughts and feelings within the poet, but of a vast and general ideal world of which the real world is merely an imperfect representation. This concept of the existence of an ideal world lying beyond reality which was popularized by the eighteenth-century philosopher, Swedenborg, goes back, of course, at least to Plato, and plays its part in Christianity, but it was not until the nineteenth century, when the decline in Christian belief was accompanied by a search for other ways of escaping from the harsh world of reality, that the idea was conceived of this other world being attainable, not through mysticism or religion, but through the medium of poetry. 'C'est par et à travers la poésie', said Baudelaire in his *Notes Nouvelles sur Edgar Poe*, 'que l'âme entrevoit les splendeurs situées derrière le tombeau' – 'it is through and by means of poetry that the soul perceives the splendours lying beyond the grave' – and he went on to say that when a perfect poem brings tears to the eyes, this is evidence of the fact that the reader feels himself exiled in an imperfect world and longs to break out from it into the paradise that has been revealed to him – 'c'est le témoignage d'une nature exilée dans l'imparfait et qui voudrait s'emparer immédiatement sur cette terre même, d'un paradis révélé'. It was Baudelaire and his successors who elevated the poet to the rank of priest or prophet or what Rimbaud called 'le poète-voyant' – 'the poet-seer' – endowed with the power to see behind and beyond the objects of the real world to the essences concealed in the ideal world. The purpose of poetry became to create for the reader this world outside reality by a subtle transformation of reality as we know it. Mallarmé defined this goal in a well-known passage in which he claimed that he created in his poetry not any real flower but 'l'absente de tous bouquets', the essential flower which is not to be found among any of the flowers of the world below. The whole purpose of poetry, he said in another famous phrase, was to create, 'sans la gêne d'un proche ou concret rappel, la notion pure' – pure essences, unhindered by any echo of the concrete reality which surrounds us.

But although the aim of the transcendental Symbolist is to go beyond reality he must obviously, like the human Symbolist, use reality as his starting-point and it is in order to make the transition from the real to the ideal that the imagery in Symbolist poetry of this kind is so often obscure or confused. This is a deliberate blurring so that the reader's eye can focus beyond reality on the essential Idea (to use the Platonic term much favoured by the Symbolists) of which the various symbols are partial and inadequate manifestations. To take just a single example, based on the one Mallarmé himself used – if the poet wants to present to the reader the ideal flower, he must not draw too clearly the specific image of a rose or a lily, but must confuse the two images so that the essence of them both may be perceived. Mallarmé's own magnificent and virtually untranslatable definition of this process, part of which has already been quoted, runs as follows: 'Je dis: une fleur! et, hors de l'oubli où ma voix relègue aucun contour, en tant que quelque chose d'autre que les calices sus, musicalement se lève, idée même et suave, l'absente de tous bouquets' (*Œuvres Complètes*, p. 857). Mallarmé, therefore, starts from reality, but any tangible flower is consigned to oblivion and something other than a 'known calyx', rises from this oblivion, the perfect Idea of a flower, the 'absente de tous bouquets' that has already been referred to.

It is significant that in this passage Mallarmé uses the adverb 'musicalement', because one of the tenets of Symbolism, both of the human and of the transcendental kind, that further help to define its meaning more closely, was the equation between poetry and music in preference to the equation between poetry and sculpture, or poetry and painting that had been current in the middle of the nineteenth century in France. The reason for this belief that, as Walter Pater put it in his essay on Giorgione published in 1873, 'all art aspires towards the condition of music', was that music possesses just that quality of suggestiveness that the Symbolists were looking for, and lacks just that element of precision which words necessarily possess and which the Symbolists wished to suppress. 'De la musique avant toute chose', is the celebrated command with which Verlaine's *Art Poétique*, written in 1874, begins, and it ends with a peremptory dismissal of everything that does not possess this vague, suggestive, musical quality as mere literature: 'Et tout le reste est littérature' (*Oeuvres Complètes*, p. 207), echoing Rimbaud's equally peremptory dismissal, in a letter written three years before, of the whole of French poetry: 'Tout est prose rimée.' Paul Valéry, who can perhaps be considered as the last of the Symbolists, expresses a similar idea when he defines Symbolism in an essay on Baudelaire (*Oeuvres Complètes*, pp. 611–12) as being simply the desire shown by several poets to 'reprendre à la musique leur bien' – to take back from music what really belonged to them – an idea which Mallarmé had already expressed the other way around in an essay on Wagner whom he had described as 'usurping the duty of the poet' (*Oeuvres Complètes*, p. 541).

It was because of this desire to attain the fluidity of music that Symbolist poetry so often refused to conform to the rigid conventions as regards versification which, despite the earlier revolutionary efforts of the Romantic poets, still held sway in France. The kind and the degree of freedom practised by the Symbolist poets varies of course with the individual – the earliest of them, Baudelaire, was no great innovator in this respect and Verlaine was scarcely bold enough to go beyond 'vers libérés' – freed verse – to 'vers libres' – free verse. Rimbaud, on the other hand, soon went far beyond these modest attempts to liberate French poetry from the shackles of the traditional patterns of rhyme and rhythm and he adopted the form of the prose poem. As for Mallarmé although he appears for the most part to work within a conventional framework, he is in fact as great a revolutionary as Rimbaud in his paradoxically discreet way and in the last months of his life in 1898 he wrote *Un Coup de Dés* (*Oeuvres Complètes*, pp. 455–77), the originality of which has probably never been equalled by anything written since.

Symbolism can, then, be finally said to be an attempt to penetrate beyond reality to a world of ideas, either the ideas within the poet, including his emotions, or the Ideas in the Platonic sense that constitute a perfect supernatural world towards which man aspires. In order to thus get behind the surface of reality there is often a fusion of images, a kind of stereoscopic effect to give a third dimension. Great emphasis is also laid on the musical quality of poetry (which Valéry in fact defined as 'cette hésitation prolongée entre le son et le sens' – 'this constant hovering between sound and sense') and, because of the wish to achieve a greater flexibility, the regular rhythm of the twelve-syllable alexandrine, for example, and the recurring pattern of conventional rhyme schemes were discarded.

It was along these lines that Symbolism, which had slowly been shaping an identity for itself, was in fact defined in a manifesto published by Jean Moréas in an article in the newspaper *Le Figaro* on 18 September 1886. In it, he claimed that Romanticism had had its day, that its successors, the Parnassian movement in poetry and the Naturalist movement in the novel were also at an end, and that a new form of art was awaited and was indeed necessary and inevitable. He defined the new movement as being against the purveying of information, against declamation, against false sensibility and against objective description. Instead, he declared its aim to be the attempt to give outward form to Ideas (and he clearly means this term to be taken in the Platonic sense) – 'la poésie symbolique

cherche à vêtir l'Idée d'une forme sensible.' Among the leaders of
the new movement he named Baudelaire as 'le véritable précurseur'
and praised Mallarmé for having given to it 'le sens du mystère et
de l'ineffable', while Verlaine's contribution he defined as having
been 'to break the cruel bonds of versification'. Rimbaud's absence
from this list may seem surprising, but it is no doubt explained by
the fact that his reputation had barely begun to be established at
that date.

But although Moréas thus acknowledged that by 1886 Symbolism already existed and that he was simply proclaiming the fact
to the public at large, at the same time he considered his manifesto
to be a programme for the future and he founded the 'école symboliste' in which he was joined by such figures as René Ghil,
Stuart Merrill, Francis Viélé-Griffin and Gustave Kahn. It is
this that has given rise to a certain confusion since there are some
critics who regard Symbolism as synonymous with the Symbolist
school and who consequently devote considerable space to the
very minor poets belonging to the latter and relegate Baudelaire,
Verlaine, Rimbaud and Mallarmé to the rank of mere precursors
of the Symbolist movement. Other critics, however, recognize the
futility of wasting a useful and convenient critical term on minor
poets and of thus leaving four major poets in a kind of limbo,
belonging to none of the three great movements which dominated
nineteenth-century French poetry, the Romantic movement, the
Parnassian movement and the Symbolist movement.

2

Baudelaire's 'Correspondances'

The double Symbolist concept that reality is no more than a façade, concealing either a world of ideas and emotions within the poet, or an ideal world towards which he aspires, is associated in the case of Baudelaire with the doctrine outlined in his celebrated sonnet *Correspondances*. Sensations, for Baudelaire, are not merely sensations; they can convey thoughts or feelings of, for example, corruption, wealth or triumph:

> Il est des parfums . . . .
> . . . corrompus, riches et triomphants

and objects are not simply objects but are the symbols of ideal forms lying concealed behind them:

> La Nature est un temple où de vivants piliers
> Laissent parfois sortir de confuses paroles.
> L'homme y passe à travers des forêts de symboles . . .

There are a number of poems in Baudelaire's one volume of poetry, *Les Fleurs du Mal*, first published in 1857 and followed three years later by a second, considerably enlarged edition, which illustrate the first of these two related concepts. *Harmonie du Soir*, for example, might appear at first reading to be simply a description of a landscape since it consists almost entirely of a series of images – the setting sun, the fading perfume of flowers, the dying note of a violin:

> Voici venir les temps où vibrant sur sa tige
> Chaque fleur s'évapore ainsi qu'un encensoir;
> Les sons et les parfums tournent dans l'air du soir;
> Valse mélancolique et langoureux vertige.

Chaque fleur s'évapore ainsi qu'un encensoir;
Le violon frémit comme un coeur qu'on afflige;
Valse mélancolique et langoureux vertige!
Le ciel est triste et beau comme un grand reposoir.

Le violon frémit comme un coeur qu'on afflige,
Un coeur tendre qui hait le néant vaste et noir!
Le ciel est triste et beau comme un grand reposoir;
Le soleil s'est noyé dans son sang qui se fige.

Un coeur tendre qui hait le néant vaste et noir,
Du passé lumineux recueille tout vestige!
Le soleil s'est noyé dans son sang qui se fige . . .
Ton souvenir en moi luit comme un ostensoir!

(Now come the days when, trembling on its stem,
Each flower is scented like an incense bowl;
Sounds and perfumes swirl through the evening air;
The senses turn in a slow and languid dance.

Each flower is scented like an incense bowl;
A violin trembles like a broken heart;
The senses turn in a slow and languid dance;
The sky is sad and splendid like an altar.

A violin trembles like a broken heart,
A loving heart that hates the vast and dark abyss;
The sky is sad and splendid like an altar;
The sun has sunk in its own congealing blood.

A loving heart that hates the vast and dark abyss
Gathers every vestige of the hallowed past;
The sun has sunk in its own congealing blood . . .
My memory of you gleams like a sacred shrine.)

The final line, however, 'Ton souvenir en moi luit comme un ostensoir', provides the clue indicating that these repeated images, all possessing as a common factor the notion of something beauti-

B

ful that has passed away, are in fact objective correlatives whose purpose is to re-create in the reader the emotion experienced by the poet at the memory of a past love affair.

Precisely the same process is followed, though in order to re-create a very different emotion, in the first of the four poems entitled *Spleen* where all the images again have a common factor though it is quite unlike that of *Harmonie du Soir*:

> Pluvîose, irrité contre la ville entière,
> De son urne à grands flots verse un froid ténébreux
> Aux pâles habitants du voisin cimetière
> Et la mortalité sur les faubourgs brumeux.
>
> Mon chat sur le carreau cherchant une litière
> Agite sans repos son corps maigre et galeux;
> L'âme d'un vieux poète erre dans la gouttière
> Avec la triste voix d'un fantôme frileux.
>
> Le bourdon se lamente et la bûche enfumée
> Accompagne en fausset la pendule enrhumée,
> Cependant qu'en un jeu plein de sales parfums,
>
> Héritage fatale d'une vieille hydropique
> Le beau valet de coeur et la dame de pique
> Causent sinistrement de leurs amours défunts.
>
> (The god of rain, in anger against the city,
> Pours down floods of cold and darkness
> On the pale inhabitants of the nearby cemetery
> And waves of death on the fog-ridden suburbs.
>
> My cat, trying to find a place to rest,
> Twists and turns his thin and sickly body;
> The soul of an old poet haunts the rooftops
> With the sad voice of a trembling ghost.
>
> The church bell tolls and the smoking log
> Hisses alongside the wheezing clock,
> While in a stale-smelling pack of playing cards,

A gloomy legacy from a crippled old hag,
The handsome Knave of Hearts and the Queen of Spades
Coldly talk about their long-dead love.)

Once more it is the final line, and even the last two words, which
provide the clue as to what the poem is really about. It is only then
that one fully realizes that the purpose of all the preceding images
in their various ways is to make the reader feel the cold hand of
death that has descended on the love affair between the knave of
hearts and the queen of spades who can be taken to represent
Baudelaire and his coloured mistress Jeanne Duval, dragging out a
miserable existence long after the relationship between them had
ceased to have any warmth and any real meaning. Far from being a
mere description of a sad and mournful scene *Spleen* is therefore an
attempt and, in its own way, as successful an attempt as *Harmonie
du Soir*, to re-create in the reader, through an accumulation of
symbols, an emotion experienced by the poet.

Human Symbolism of this sort plays a considerable part in
Baudelaire's poetry, but perhaps an even more important part is
played by transcendental Symbolism. To some extent the two
overlap in that *Harmonie du Soir*, for example, may be said to evoke
not only a feeling of perfect happiness but also, at least by implica-
tion, a picture of paradise. Similarly *Spleen* may be regarded as depicting a scene from hell (a kind of hell that heralds in some degree
Sartre's *Huis Clos*) as well as conveying a mood of black despair.
Other poems, however, lay greater stress on the transcendental
aspect of Symbolism and endeavour to penetrate beyond reality to
an ideal world. In *La Chevelure*, for example, it is not Jeanne
Duval's hair that really fascinates Baudelaire, nor the fact that its
jet-black colour and wavy texture remind him of a voyage he had
made shortly before through the Indian Ocean to Mauritius:

La langoureuse Asie et la brûlante Afrique,
Tout un monde absent, lointain, presque défunt
Vit dans tes profondeurs, forêt aromatique . . .

This is not simply a case of present reality nostalgically recalling past reality. Had Baudelaire really wanted to return to the tropics, his family, who had insisted on his making his original voyage in the hope of calling a halt to the Bohemian life he had begun to lead in Paris, would no doubt have been only too glad to send him there. What he is really looking for is a non-existent paradise and it is this for which he finds a symbol in a past memory concealed within a present reality. Once more there is a common factor to the various images in the poem and what they transmit to the reader is the notion of eternity and infinity, conveyed by such expressions as 'tout un monde absent, lointain, presque défunt', 'un éblouissant rêve', 'un ciel pur où frémit l'éternelle chaleur', 'infinis bercements', 'l'azur du ciel immense et rond' and 'l'oasis où je rêve'.

An even more idealized picture of a future paradise is presented in *L'Invitation au Voyage* where this time the objective correlative of Baudelaire's immaterial world is a Dutch landscape, though he had never in fact been to Holland, and still more perhaps than in *La Chevelure* there is a certain quality of eternity and infinity about the phrasing, especially the refrain three times repeated:

> Là, tout n'est qu'ordre et beauté,
> Luxe, calme et volupté.

Elsewhere he looks back with longing towards his childhood and to what he calls in *Moesta et Errabunda* 'Le vert paradis des amours enfantines', yet another guise under which the ideal world appears in *Les Fleurs du Mal*.

In giving poetic form to these various symbolic representations of paradise Baudelaire is escaping from reality through the medium of poetry. He is in fact creating a kind of second reality and his distant, absent world, his dazzling dream, his pure skies shimmering with eternal warmth, his land of order and beauty, luxury, calm and voluptuousness reside in his poetry which fixes this ideal world not only for the poet himself but also for his readers.

Thus the poet becomes a divine figure, able to see through the wall of reality to the paradise beyond and able to transmit his vision to others. He is endowed with the capacity, as the poem *Elévation* puts it, to understand 'le langage des fleurs et des choses muettes'. He does in fact belong by nature to this paradise and is an exiled figure here on earth according to *Bénédiction*, the opening poem of *Les Fleurs du Mal*, which makes an almost explicit analogy between the poet and Christ and is closely linked with other poems in *Les Fleurs du Mal* which stress the angelic nature and divine mission of art and the artist.

These essentially optimistic poems are, however, virtually limited to the first few in *Les Fleurs du Mal*, and although the long opening section is entitled *Spleen et Idéal*, the movement of this section is actually in the opposite direction, from 'idéal' to 'spleen', from a supremely optimistic belief that a paradise exists beyond the real world and can be perceived and re-created by the poet, to a profoundly pessimistic recognition that reality may not, after all, be a 'correspondance du ciel' but rather a 'correspondance de l'enfer'. 'C'est le diable qui tient les fils qui nous remuent' – 'it is the devil who pulls the strings which control us' – contends Baudelaire in the poem *Au Lecteur* which serves as a preface to his volume and warns the reader that the optimism of the first few poems will soon be dissipated. By the time he has neared the end of *Spleen et Idéal* he no longer conceives of himself as a divine being for whom a place is reserved in heaven, as he had done in *Bénédiction* but as:

> Une Idée, une Forme, un Etre
> Parti de l'azur et tombé
> Dans un Styx bourbeux et plombé
> Où nul œil du ciel ne pénètre.

Reality no longer conceals a radiant paradise but a gloomy inferno which Baudelaire now glimpses, not only in a poem such as *Spleen*, but more clearly in, for example, *Les Sept Vieillards* where a terrifying procession of seven crippled old men appear to him out of hell.

At the end of *Les Fleurs du Mal* Baudelaire is thus no longer sure exactly what is the nature of the world lying beyond reality. In the final verse of the closing poem, *Le Voyage*, when his one desire is to bring to an end his journey through life, defined in retrospect as 'une oasis d'horreur dans un désert d'ennui', he acknowledges that it is to an unknown destination that he will be setting off, that it may be either heaven or hell that is awaiting him:

> Plonger au fond du gouffre, Enfer ou Ciel, qu'importe,
> Au fond de l'inconnu pour trouver du nouveau.

Both transcendental Symbolism and human Symbolism form part of what have been called 'correspondances verticales' involving movement from the plane of material objects and the sensations they provoke to the plane of abstract concepts and personal feelings, from sights and sounds and smells to the notions or emotions they inspire. There also exist, however, in Baudelaire's poetry, what have been called 'correspondances horizontales' or movements on the same plane from one physical sensation to another. In the lines from the sonnet *Correspondances* that have been quoted, Baudelaire not only contends that perfumes can be 'corrompus, riches et triomphants', he also claims that:

> Les parfums, les couleurs et les sons se répondent.
> Il est des parfums frais comme des chairs d'enfant,
> Doux comme les hautbois, verts comme les prairies.

Perfumes can therefore have the same quality as the soft feel of children's flesh, or as the gentle sound of oboes, or as the green colour of fields. This process of sense transference, or synaesthesia, has often been remarked upon in *Les Fleurs du Mal*, especially in those poems addressed to Jeanne Duval where the perfume of her hair stimulates visual images of tropical lands, or the sound of ships in distant harbours. But this correspondence between the different senses is in fact no more than a variation on the general process of repetition that is fundamental to Baudelaire's poetry and which brings it close to music. Since his aim is not to tell a story or to define an idea, but to create an emotion or to convey an impression, he accumulates outward symbols which constantly reiterate and reinforce the essential inner theme of the poem. An obvious way of doing this and, at the same time, of avoiding monotony, is to find images belonging to the different senses, rather as a composer calls in the different instruments of an orchestra. But there is no basic difference between, on the one hand, *Harmonie du Soir*, for example, where a feeling of past happiness and the impression of a paradise lost are conveyed through images which make a threefold appeal to the sense of smell, the sense of hearing and the sense of sight, and, on the other hand, the last three verses of *Le Cygne* where a feeling of captivity and the impression of a world without hope are conveyed through an accumulation of images that are entirely visual:

> Je pense à la négresse, amaigrie et phtisique,
> Piétinant dans la boue, et cherchant, l'œil hagard
> Les cocotiers absents de la superbe Afrique
> Derrière la muraille immense du brouillard;
>
> A quiconque a perdu ce qui ne se retrouve
> Jamais, jamais! à ceux qui s'abreuvent de pleurs
> Et tettent la Douleur comme une bonne louve!
> Aux maigres orphelins séchant comme des fleurs!
>
> Ainsi dans la forêt où mon esprit s'exile
> Un vieux Souvenir sonne à plein souffle du cor!
> Je pense aux matelots oubliés dans une île,
> Aux captifs, aux vaincus! . . . à bien d'autres encor!

(I remember the thin, consumptive negress
Trudging through the mud and looking, weary eyed,
For the long-lost palm trees of proud Africa
Beyond the endless prison-wall of fog.

I think of all those who have lost something
Forever and forever; of those who drink their tears
And are suckled by sorrow as their foster-mother.
I think of orphans as shrunken as dried flowers.

Thus in the dense forest where my mind roams,
An old memory echoes like a hunting horn.
I think of sailors lost on desert islands,
Of captives, of prisoners and of many more . . .)

It was no doubt this Baudelairian characteristic of insistently repeating the same thing in various guises, not infrequently with an actual system of refrains, as in *Harmonie du Soir*, that led the leading nineteenth-century French critic, Ferdinand Brunetière, to say of him disparagingly: 'Ses vers suent l'effort. Ce qu'il voudrait dire, il est très rare qu'il le dise. Le pauvre diable n'avait rien, ou presque rien du poète que la rage de le devenir.' ('His lines reek of straining after effect. He rarely manages to say what he is trying to say. The poor devil had nothing of the poet about him except the desperate longing to become one.') It is true that Brunetière revised this judgement in later years, but it is a measure of the originality of *Les Fleurs du Mal* that one of the authoritative literary figures of the day should at first have so signally failed to understand and appreciate the Symbolist approach to poetry.

3
Verlaine's melodies

Paul Verlaine, born in 1844, a generation after Baudelaire, and just beginning his career as a poet when the latter was at the height of his fame, could not help but be influenced by *Les Fleurs du Mal* to some extent. All the more so because his temperament and psychological make-up were not unlike Baudelaire's in that both had enjoyed a sheltered, and even over-sheltered, childhood and that both found the harsh reality of the adult world increasingly hard to bear. Baudelaire's shift from optimism to pessimism is, however, a fairly steady one – at least as it is presented in *Les Fleurs du Mal*, although in real life the transition was no doubt much more irregular. Whereas both in Verlaine's life and in his work there is a constant swaying to and fro from the darkest despair to the most radiant optimism, from the sadness of the 'paysages tristes' in *Poèmes Saturniens* to the joy and confidence of *La Bonne Chanson*, from the vague melancholy of the 'ariettes oubliées' in *Romances sans Paroles* to the firm and clear resolution of many of the poems of *Sagesse*.

But whatever mood Verlaine may be in he practises Baudelaire's principle – at least in his best poetry – of conveying rather than describing it, and he does so by the same method of using an outward symbol that 'corresponds' to his inner emotion. Just as Baudelaire had said in *Le Cygne* that the rebuilding of the Louvre, the scaffolding around it, and the blocks of stone all had a hidden significance for him:

> ... palais neufs, échafaudages, blocs,
> Vieux faubourgs, tout pour moi devient allégorie,

so Verlaine in *Romances sans Paroles* acknowledges, as he wanders through a misty countryside, that it reflects his own sadness:

> Combien, ô voyageur, ce paysage blême
> Te mira blême toi-même.

Like *Harmonie du Soir* and *Spleen*, many of Verlaine's poems are apparently descriptive, save for some slight indication that their true purpose is rather different, as with the following landscape from *La Bonne Chanson* where only the detached line at the end of each verse indicates that there are two people involved and that it is in fact a tender love poem:

La lune blanche	(The pale moon
Luit dans les bois	Shines through the trees
De chaque branche	From each branch
Part une voix	A song murmurs
Sous la ramée . . .	Beneath the leaves
O bien-aimée.	O my loved one.
L'étang reflète,	The pond reflects
Profond miroir,	Like a deep mirror
La silhouette	The silhouette
Du saule noir	Of the dark willow
Où le vent pleure . . .	Where the wind weeps
Rêvons, c'est l'heure.	The hour to dream has come.
Un vaste et tendre	A vast and tender
Apaisement	Peacefulness
Semble descendre	Seems to descend
Du firmament	From the firmament
Que l'astre irise . . .	Lit by the setting sun
C'est l'heure exquise.	The hour of happiness has come.)

Though the emotion conveyed is very different, fundamentally the same method is used in one of the religious sonnets of *Sagesse* where Verlaine plays on the literal and metaphorical senses of the word 'day' (one might almost say the meteorological and chronological senses) and by depicting a physical storm conveys the feeling of the spiritual storm taking place in him as he struggles against temptation:

> Les faux beaux jours ont lui tout le jour, ma pauvre âme,
> Et les voici vibrer aux cuivres du couchant...
> Ils ont lui tout le jour en longs grêlons de flamme,
> Battant tout vendange aux collines, couchant
> Toute moisson de la vallée, et ravageant
> Le ciel bleu, le ciel chanteur qui te réclame...

> (The false good old days have shone all day, my poor soul
> And now they ring out in the copper coloured sunset...
> They have shone all day in shafts of lightning and hail
> Beating down the harvest in the hills, laying flat
> The harvest in the valley and sweeping away
> The blue sky, the singing sky that summons you...)

In these and many other of his best and best-known poems, such as *Soleils Couchants, Chanson d'Automne, Le Piano que Baise une Main Frêle, Dans l'Interminable Ennui de la Plaine*, and *Le Ciel est, par-dessus le Toit*, Verlaine thus practises the same kind of human Symbolism as Baudelaire. But he differs from Baudelaire in that the transcendental aspect of Symbolism is largely absent from his work. Even at those moments when he optimistically looks forward to a new kind of life vastly different from reality as it then was (in the poems of *La Bonne Chanson*, for example, written just before his marriage, or in those poems of *Sagesse* written immediately after his return to Catholicism) Verlaine's attitude remains an essentially emotional one. He lacked Baudelaire's imaginative power and his ability to create a picture of the paradise awaiting him. Indeed when Verlaine tries to do this, his poems all too often collapse into utter banality; they cease, in fact, to be Symbolist poems and instead of trying to convey the impression of another world they simply state that it exists and try to analyse and describe the means by which it is to be attained in the most trivial fashion, as in one of the least successful of the many unsuccessful poems of *La Bonne Chanson*:

> Oui, je veux marcher droit et calme dans la Vie
> Vers le but où le sort dirigera mes pas;
> Sans violence, sans remords, et sans envie:
> Ce sera le devoir heureux aux gais combats.
>
> Et comme, pour bercer les lenteurs de la route
> Je chanterai des airs ingénus, je me dis
> Qu'elle m'écoutera sans déplaisir sans doute;
> Et vraiment je ne veux pas d'autre Paradis.
>
> (Yes, I shall march firmly and calmly through Life
> Towards the goal where fate will direct my steps,
> Without violence, without remorse and without envy
> Happy to do my duty in the cheerful struggle.
>
> And since, to while away time on life's road
> I shall sing simple songs, I tell myself
> That she will listen to me with pleasure
> And that is the only Paradise I desire.)

The gulf that separates platitudes of this sort from a poem such as Baudelaire's *La Chevelure* is clearly enormous, although no greater than the gulf that separates them from those poems by Verlaine himself that have already been mentioned in which he makes no attempt to build up a sustained picture of another world in a quasi-Baudelairian manner, but simply indulges his own particular and peculiar genius for conveying his own feelings in a few swift and telling strokes which sketch out the objective correlative of those feelings.

A second difference between Baudelaire and Verlaine is that although the latter adopts a similar technique of repetition, of circling round the feeling he is trying to put across, here too he lacks Baudelaire's breadth and richness. This does not mean that Verlaine's poetry is any less musical than Baudelaire's, but whereas the latter's music tends to be splendidly orchestrated with the different senses called in to play their part at carefully chosen moments, images amply developed, lines evenly balanced and assonance and alliteration used in an overt though effective fashion, Verlaine's poetry has a much more subtle and intimate kind of melody. A comparison between Baudelaire's *Harmonie du Soir*, quoted on pp. 8–9, and the following poem by Verlaine on a not dissimilar theme clearly illustrates the difference between the two poets in this respect:

Une aube affaiblie	(A pale dawn light
Verse par les champs	Creeps over the fields
La mélancolie	With all the sadness
Des soleils couchants.	Of setting suns.
La mélancolie	All the sadness
Berce de doux chants	Soothes with songs
Mon coeur qui s'oublie	My heart which sinks
Aux soleils couchants.	With setting suns.
Et d'étranges rêves,	And strange dreams,
Comme des soleils	Like setting
Couchants sur les grèves,	Suns over shores,
Fantômes vermeils,	Like crimson ghosts,
Défilent sans trêves,	Ceaselessly wheel,
Défilent, pareils	Wheel like
A de grands soleils	Huge setting
Couchants sur les grèves.	Suns over shores.)

Here there is no more than a hint of 'correspondances horizontales' between setting suns and soothing songs, and it remains undeveloped. The light at sunset is compared briefly to the light at dawn, but there is no such splendid image as the one used by Baudelaire: 'Le soleil s'est noyé dans son sang qui se fige.' The careful and complex system of refrains in *Harmonie du Soir* gives way to the seemingly casual repetition of 'la mélancolie' in lines 3 and 5 and of 'défilent' at the beginning of lines 13 and 14. Any impression of a refrain that the expression 'soleils couchants', four times repeated, might have had is suppressed by the position of the two words being altered in the last half of the poem where they are split between two lines. The slow, metronomic beat of the alexandrines in Baudelaire's poem is replaced by a quicker, irregular rhythm, due to the short, five-syllable lines and the way in which many of them are so closely linked grammatically that they cannot be separated rhythmically.

It was this extraordinarily casual and even conversational tone, which nevertheless achieves the same build-up of emotion as the measured and stately tone of *Les Fleurs du Mal*, that gave Verlaine's poetry its extreme originality at the time it was written. He had begun as a Parnassian poet and had in fact produced one of the best-known formulations of the Parnassian credo in the epilogue to his first volume, *Poèmes Saturniens*, in 1866, with its rhetorical question:

> Est-elle en marbre ou non, la Vénus de Milo?

But he soon became renowned not for the clarity of line and fullness of form that he had at first tried, not without some success, to achieve, but for the hesitant, fluid kind of poetry of *Romances sans Paroles* whose very title, borrowed from Mendelssohn's *Songs without Words*, suggests that the simplicity of these poems is such that it is not their meaning which matters but their strangely fleeting rhythms and the sense of sadness and insecurity thus conveyed.

Although Moréas saw this 'breaking of the cruel bonds of versification' as Verlaine's principal contribution to Symbolism, and although it appears, in the perspective of history, as a further appreciable step in the movement away from the traditional forms of French poetry that characterizes the whole of the nineteenth century, Verlaine was never bold enough to break with these forms completely. It is true that he dismissed rhyme in his *Art Poétique* as a mere trinket – a 'bijou d'un sou' – and that he considerably reduced the dominant rôle that it had played in, for example, Baudelaire's verse, but he never went so far as to abandon it completely and in fact in his later years he reaffirmed his belief that rhyme was essential to French poetry. With rhythm too, although he completely abandoned the sonnet form and almost completely abandoned the twelve-syllable alexandrine in his second, third and fourth volumes, *Fêtes Galantes*, *La Bonne Chanson*, and *Romances sans Paroles*, published in 1869, 1872 and 1874 respectively, and although he praised and practised the use of the unusual 'vers impair' – the line with an uneven number of syllables – as being

> Plus vague et plus soluble dans l'air
> Sans rien en lui qui pèse ou qui pose,

he never went beyond this to the use of lines of an irregular length in an irregular pattern, or to the abandonment of versification altogether. He was still enough of a traditionalist to feel that, although verse is not, of course, always poetry, poetry is, nevertheless, always verse, and it was left to his revolutionary friend Rimbaud to demonstrate that this is not in fact the case.

4
Rimbaud the 'voyant'

Rimbaud's meteoric career as a poet began in 1870 before he was sixteen and was over by 1875 before he was twenty-one. Yet in the space of those few short years he leapt from being almost as conventional a poet as Verlaine had been in his Parnassian days, to being so much a member of the 'avant-garde' that even now, a century later, his poems have a decidedly modern ring about them.

As early as May 1871, less than six months after he had published his first poem, Rimbaud wrote to one of his friends his celebrated 'lettre du voyant' in the course of which, as has already been mentioned on p. 5, he condemned the whole of French poetry as mere 'rhymed prose', dismissed Lamartine as being strangled by the out-of-date form of his poetry and even condemned his hero Baudelaire for having been too consciously artistic. What he wanted was new forms of poetry that would give freer rein to the poet's genius. 'JE est un autre', he wrote in a much-quoted phrase which is sometimes misunderstood although Rimbaud goes on to clarify it by saying that his task is to stand aside, watching and listening to the unfolding of his thought – 'j'assiste à l'éclosion de ma pensée, je la regarde, je l'écoute'. Thus the poet's function is not consciously and voluntarily to create poetry, but to allow it to develop on its own. Pushed to its extreme this principle leads in practice to Surrealism, and Rimbaud is indeed regarded as the fountainhead of this movement which developed in the early part of the twentieth century. But in the 'lettre du voyant' he is not expressing a fully worked-out theory so much as that vague feeling of discontent with discipline of every kind characteristic of someone of his age.

Although this discontent bore little or no immediate fruit, the ground was prepared for the influence of Verlaine to exercise the maximum effect when the latter invited Rimbaud to Paris in September 1871. From that date on, Rimbaud 'broke the cruel bonds of versification', to apply Moréas's phrase to him instead of to Verlaine, at an astonishing rate. In a group of poems written in May 1872 he has already far out-distanced Verlaine in the matter of technical innovations. He not only uses lines with uneven numbers of syllables, like Verlaine, but goes further and mixes lines of several different lengths, as in the poem *Bonne Pensée du Matin* which has lines of four, six, eight, nine, ten and twelve syllables in a completely irregular pattern. Rhyme too is treated with an equal nonchalance in a poem such as *Larme* where, since he cannot hit on a rhyme for 'auberge', he makes do with 'perche' and decides that 'coquillages' is an adequate echo of 'vierges' and that 'noisetiers' will suffice as a very approximate rhyme for 'villageoises'. In one poem, *Bannières de Mai*, he abandons even the last vestiges of rhyme and writes blank verse, which has never been a feature of French poetry because the unstressed nature of the French language means that there are no strong rhythmic patterns to be exploited as in English.

It was no doubt for this reason that Rimbaud moved over to prose in his *Illuminations* which he began to write later in 1872 and in most of which all trace of rhyme and of any uniform rhythm has disappeared. Rimbaud achieves his poetic effects instead by piling brilliant and unexpected images one on top of the other and by creating changing rhythmic patterns that ebb and flow with the movement of the passage as in this final paragraph from *Génie* depicting a divine figure leading his people to another world:

Il nous a connus tous, et nous a tous aimés. Sachons, cette nuit d'hiver, de cap en cap, du pôle tumultueux au château, de la foule à la plage, de regards en regards, forces et sentiments las, le héler et le voir, et le renvoyer, et sous les marées et au haut des déserts de neige, suivre ses vues, ses souffles, son corps, son jour.

(He has known us all and has loved us all. Let us then, this winter night, from cape to cape, from the Arctic wastes to the castle, from the crowd to the beach, from glance to glance, weary in strength and feeling, hail him and see him and send him forward, and beneath the seas and on the tops of the deserts of snow, follow his sight, his breath, his body, his life.)

Rimbaud was not the first to have tried to write 'prose poems'. Baudelaire notably, in his *Spleen de Paris*, otherwise known as *Petits Poèmes en Prose*, had aimed at writing what he called 'une prose poétique, musicale sans rhythme et sans rime, assez souple et assez heurté pour s'adapter aux mouvements lyriques de l'âme, aux ondulations de la rêverie, aux soubresauts de la conscience'. (A poetic prose, musical though without rhythm and without rhyme, both supple enough and hesitant enough to adapt itself to the lyrical movements of the soul, the gentle, wave-like movements of one's rêveries, the sudden leaps of one's mind.) But Baudelaire's prose poems are almost self-consciously poetic and composed with obvious care in rounded sentences, as at the beginning of *Un Hémisphère dans une Chevelure* which, like several of the *Petits Poèmes en Prose*, is a second version of a subject treated in *Les Fleurs du Mal*:

Laisse-moi respirer longtemps, longtemps, l'odeur de tes cheveux, y plonger tout mon visage, comme un homme altéré dans l'eau d'une source, et les agiter avec ma main comme un mouchoir odorant, pour secouer des souvenirs dans l'air.

(Let me breathe in for a long, long time the perfume of your hair; let me bury my head in it as a man consumed with thirst plunges his face into the waters of a stream, and let it run through my hands like a perfumed handkerchief, so as to release a wave of memories into the air.)

This ample, even leisurely phrasing with its carefully thought-out comparisons is clearly different from the direct and compelling language that Rimbaud uses, not only in the *Illuminations* but also in *Une Saison en Enfer*, as in these lines from the beginning of the final section of *Adieu*:

> L'automne déjà! – Mais pourquoi regretter un éternel soleil si nous sommes engagés à la découverte de la clarté divine, – loin des gens qui meurent sur les saisons.

> (Autumn already! – But why regret the departure of the eternal sun if we are embarked upon the discovery of a divine source of light, – far from those who die with the seasons.)

It was with this kind of writing that Rimbaud completed the Symbolist revolt against traditional versification and gave to poetry a new kind of strength and directness that made it a more fitting vehicle for the evocation of feelings and ideas. For it was as much his purpose as it was Baudelaire's and Verlaine's, once he had broken away from the conventional kind of poetry he wrote during the first few months of his career, to convey, rather than to describe, his emotions and his impressions. And what better way could be found of expressing the notion of ecstatic happiness, the sense of walking on air, the feeling of being without a care in the world, than this simple little prose poem which, with its closely related rhythmic groups, is not yet too far removed from blank verse:

> J'ai tendu des cordes de clocher à clocher; des guirlandes de fenêtre à fenêtre; des chaînes d'or d'étoile à étoile, et je danse.

> (I have stretched cords from spire to spire; garlands from window to window; golden chains from star to star and I dance.)

Though typically Rimbaldian in its directness and brevity, this accumulation of unexplained images to translate an emotion is clearly related to Baudelaire's *Harmonie du Soir* and to Verlaine's *La Lune Blanche*. Similarly the prose poem *Royauté* describes the marriage of a king and queen:

> Un beau matin, chez un peuple fort doux, un homme et une femme superbes criaient sur la place publique: 'Mes amis, je veux qu'elle soit reine!' 'Je veux être reine!' Elle riait et tremblait. Il parlait aux amis de révélation, d'épreuve terminée. Ils se pâmaient l'un contre l'autre.
>
> En effet, ils furent rois toute une matinée où les tentures carminées se relevèrent sur les maisons, et toute l'après-midi, où ils s'avancèrent du côté des jardins de palmes.

> (One fine morning, among a gentle race of people, a man and a woman proclaimed in the city square: 'My friends, I want her to be queen!' 'I want to be queen!' She laughed and trembled. He talked to his friends of revelations and of ordeals endured. They came together in a long embrace.
>
> They were indeed enthroned for a whole morning when purple hangings were raised up on the houses, and for a whole afternoon when they walked through gardens full of palms.)

But, as in *Spleen* and *La Lune Blanche*, two or three words suggest that the imagery has a hidden sense and that the king and queen are Rimbaud and his disciple or, as he was later to call him, his 'compagnon d'enfer', Verlaine, striving to create an ideal world and succeeding in doing so for a brief period when they enjoyed the triumphs symbolized by the images of the purple hangings and the palms. Although a knowledge of Rimbaud's life and ideas thus extends and deepens the meaning of the poem, it can and should be appreciated, like the poems of Baudelaire and Verlaine, simply as an evocation of a passing moment of success achieved after a long struggle by two people of widely different temperament, one a forceful, confident figure, the other of a more hesitant, essentially feminine nature. Even at this level, however, it is left to the reader to interpret the symbols used and to recognize that this is not just an account of the marriage of a king and queen in some distant country.

It was not only in the domain of human Symbolism, in the realm of the emotions, that Rimbaud adopted and extended the technique used by Baudelaire and Verlaine. As regards transcendental Symbolism too, where he plays a much more important rôle than Verlaine, who entirely lacks his intellectual strength, Rimbaud never analyses in his poetry the nature of his ideal world but simply conveys it to the reader. This is the case even with one of his relatively early and relatively conventional poems which is no doubt the most celebrated of all his works, *Le Bateau Ivre*, written just before he left for Paris in September 1871 to join Verlaine. This could be read simply as an account of its travels by a personified boat drifting wildly out of control, or as an account by Rimbaud of a vivid dream. But the real meaning of *Le Bateau Ivre*, like that of Baudelaire's *La Chevelure*, lies in the extraordinary accumulation of images with a common factor that insistently build up, not a description, but an impression of the paradise the poet is seeking.

Rimbaud's paradise, however, is very different from Baudelaire's. No doubt because he was so much younger and had led so restricted a life in the oppressive atmosphere of the small town of Charleville in north-eastern France, where he had been brought up by a harsh and domineering mother, his ideal world is not the quiet and peaceful refuge that Baudelaire longs for. On the contrary, it is a world of violence and tumult and above all of total freedom. The function of the image of the boat plunging rudderless through countless seas, dancing like a cork on the waves, encountering giant serpents and sea monsters, icebergs and waterspouts, is to make the reader feel the intense excitement and almost delirious happiness Rimbaud had in fact already experienced on the two or three occasions when he had run away from home some months before. In reality these brief escapades to Paris and

Brussels had something pathetic about them since Rimbaud was forced on each occasion to come slinking back home after a few days, and no actual account of what he had done, no mere description of what he had felt could possibly have the tremendous impact of the Symbolism of *Le Bateau Ivre*:

> Je sais les cieux crevant en éclairs, et les trombes
> Et les ressacs et les courants: je sais le soir,
> L'Aube exaltée ainsi qu'un peuple de colombes,
> Et j'ai vu quelquefois ce que l'homme a cru voir!

> (I have seen skies torn by lightning, and waterspouts
> And breakers and currents; I have seen the dusk,
> And the Dawn rising like a flock of doves,
> And I have seen things that men have only imagined!)

It should be added that these were things that Rimbaud too had only imagined since at that date he had never even seen the sea. Unlike Baudelaire he did not have the resources of a wide experience of life to draw upon for his imagery. But, like Baudelaire's world of memory, his world of imagination was more real than reality itself. This is the sense of the term 'le poète voyant' – the poet who sees through to another world beyond reality. Whereas Baudelaire, however, felt that this power as a seer was a gift made to the poet, Rimbaud, on the contrary, believed that 'le poète *se fait* voyant' – 'the poet *makes himself* a seer' – and he does so by the deliberate 'derangement of the senses', as he called it, 'le long, immense, et raisonné dérèglement de tous les sens'. By subjecting himself to every form of sensual experience – 'toutes les formes d'amour, de souffrance, de folie' – he acquires a kind of hypersensitivity which enables him to see things imperceptible to others, to understand 'le langage des fleurs et des choses muettes' to quote Baudelaire's phrase. For Rimbaud too, therefore, the poet is a divine figure, able to create his own world, and just as Baudelaire had implicitly compared the poet to Christ in *Bénédiction*, so

Rimbaud is quoted by Verlaine in the latter's *Crimen Amoris* as saying: 'Je serai celui-là qui créera Dieu' – 'I shall be the one who will create God himself.' Rimbaud does indeed, in several passages of the *Illuminations*, treat reality as the raw material from which he creates a new world. In *Marine*, for example, (another poem where he has not yet moved over completely to prose and which is written in free verse with unrhymed lines of different lengths) the land is transformed into the sea and the sea into the land:

> Les chars d'argent et de cuivre –
> Les proues d'acier et d'argent –
> Battent l'écume –
> Soulèvent les souches des ronces.
> Les courants de la lande,
> Et les ornières immenses du reflux,
> Filent circulairement vers l'est,
> Vers les piliers de la forêt, –
> Vers les fûts de la jetée,
> Dont l'angle est heurté par des tourbillons de lumière.

> (The ploughs of silver and bronze –
> The prows of steel and silver –
> Push through the waves, –
> Lift up the bramble roots.
> The currents of the land,
> And the long furrows of the ebb-tide,
> Flow round towards the east,
> Towards the pillars of the forest, –
> Towards the trunks of the jetty,
> Whose corner is swept by whirlpools of light.)

'Je m'habituai à l'hallucination simple,' wrote Rimbaud in the section of *Une Saison en Enfer* entitled *Alchimie du Verbe*, 'je voyais très franchement une mosquée à la place d'une usine.' But this process of hallucination to which he accustomed himself, this capacity to see mosques in place of factories, to re-mould reality, did not last. Verlaine had played a vital part in encouraging Rimbaud in his attempt to make poetry into a creative force, but the personal relationship between them turned sour and ended in a violent quarrel in July 1873. It was then that Rimbaud wrote *Une Saison en Enfer* – *A Season in Hell* – looking back with bitterness on the previous months which were to have been, on the contrary, a season in heaven with himself playing the rôle of God the creator. What he had previously called 'the sacred disorder of my mind', he now describes as a delirium, and *Délires* is indeed the title of one of the central chapters of *Une Saison en Enfer*. Similarly the sub-title *Alchimie du Verbe*, that has already been referred to, implies that his one-time belief that the power of the word could change base metal into gold was as foolish as the dream of the medieval alchemists.

Like Baudelaire, Rimbaud thus fails in his attempt to penetrate beyond reality to an ideal world. Yet just as Baudelaire, at the end of *Le Voyage*, despite the earlier pessimism of *Spleen* and *Les Sept Vieillards*, leaves open the possibility that it may after all be attainable, that in the depths of the abyss may lie either heaven or hell, so Rimbaud, at the very end of *Une Saison en Enfer*, recovers from his despair and holds out the hope that, despite his own failure, the dawn of a new era will come and his ideal world will be reached:

Et à l'aurore, armés d'une ardente patience, nous entrerons aux splendides villes.

(And at dawn, armed with a burning patience, we shall enter the splendid cities.)

Patience, however, was just what Rimbaud lacked, and in fact one study of him is entitled *Rimbaud, ou le Génie Impatient*. But the same critic who thus described Rimbaud as 'the impatient genius' also described another poet, Stéphane Mallarmé, as possessing 'cette longue patience qui est la marque du génie' – 'that stubborn patience that is the hallmark of genius' and it was indeed Mallarmé who came nearer than any other Symbolist poet to achieving his goal and who is generally regarded as the high priest of Symbolism.

5
Mallarmé and the infinite

Mallarmé's theory of transcendental Symbolism sprang originally from the same sense of dissatisfaction with reality as his fellow Symbolists experienced, and this sense of dissatisfaction, in its turn, may well be attributable to similar causes. For it is no doubt a significant fact that, with the possible exception of Verlaine, each of these poets had a disturbed childhood – Baudelaire's father died when he was six years old, Rimbaud's father deserted his wife and family after half a dozen years of marriage, and Mallarmé's mother died when he was five years old. In one of his earliest poems, *Apparition*, where Mallarmé describes a figure with a halo of light that he remembers appearing to him in his childhood dreams and sprinkling over him clusters of perfumed stars, there is little doubt that this is an idealized image of his dead mother:

> . . . la fée au chapeau de clarté
> Qui jadis sur mes beaux sommeils d'enfant gâté
> Passait, laissant toujours de ses mains mal fermés
> Neiger de blancs bouquets d'étoiles parfumées.

These lines date from 1862 when Mallarmé was twenty and when his poetry already expressed his longing to turn his back on life, to 'tourner l'épaule à la vie' as he puts it in *Les Fenêtres*, and to be re-born into the world he has lost and still dreams of, a world where Beauty flowers:

> A renaître, portant mon rêve en diadême,
> Au ciel antérieur où fleurit la Beauté.

Thus far Mallarmé's poetry clearly resembles that of Baudelaire, but by the end of 1864, with his keen and probing mind and his need for an intellectually satisfying answer to his longings, Mallarmé found that he could not simply take refuge in some vague, exotic dream of an ideal world. If there was an alternative to reality then it must, in Mallarmé's view, be capable of rational definition. To achieve such a definition was the task Mallarmé set himself in the years 1864 and 1865 and the 'clair regard de diamant' of his cold, introspective princess, Hérodiade, who figures in the uncompleted verse drama he began at this time, symbolizes his own relentless search for the answer to his problem.

But when he thus turned the cold light of reason upon the question of the nature of the ideal world he at first arrived at the apparently obvious conclusion that beyond the real world there lies nothing but an empty void and several of his letters at this time contain allusions to 'le Néant' and to 'le Rien qui est la vérité'. Sustained, however, by his conviction that an ideal world must exist and helped perhaps by being introduced to the work of the German philosopher Hegel, he passed beyond this first conclusion to a second conclusion – that the ideal world lies hidden in the empty void, that 'l'infini' is contained within 'le néant', to use two terms which stand in opposition to each other in French much more easily than do their equivalents in English. The poet's function, therefore, is to cut himself off from all contact with reality, to create a kind of void within himself into which the ideal forms of the infinite world contained within 'le néant' will flow and crystallize. 'Je suis maintenant impersonnel', wrote Mallarmé to his friend Cazalis in 1867, 'et non plus Stéphane que tu as connu, mais une aptitude qu'a l'univers spirituel à se voir et à se développer à travers ce qui fut moi.' (I am now depersonalized; I am no longer Stéphane Mallarmé, but simply a means whereby the spiritual universe can become visible and can develop through what was once me.)

There is a curious similarity between this phrase and the one
Rimbaud used half a dozen years later when he wrote: 'JE est un
autre.' But in fact the two poets arrived at their parallel ideas quite
independently and developed them in quite different ways.
Whereas Rimbaud merely stands aside and lets his chaotic visions
flood into his mind, Mallarmé consciously empties his mind of all
images founded in reality and equally consciously builds up his
images of the 'absent flowers' and 'pure notions' referred to on p.
4 above.

This is the case with what is probably the key poem in the whole
of Mallarmé's work, the sonnet he wrote, or began to write in 1868
under the title *Sonnet Allégorique de Lui-même* and which he
finally published almost twenty years later in 1887, without a title
and with a number of alterations of a relatively minor nature:

> Ses purs ongles très haut dédiant leur onyx,
> L'Angoisse, ce minuit, soutient, lampadophore,
> Maint rêve vespéral brûlé par le Phénix
> Que ne recueille pas de cinéraire amphore
>
> Sur les crédences, au salon vide: nul ptyx,
> Aboli bibelot d'inanité sonore,
> (Car le Maître est allé puiser des pleurs au Styx
> Avec ce seul objet dont le Néant s'honore).
>
> Mais proche la croisée au nord vacante, un or
> Agonise selon peut-être le décor
> Des licornes ruant du feu contre une nixe,
>
> Elle, défunte nue en le miroir, encor
> Que, dans l'oubli fermé par le cadre, se fixe
> De scintillations sitôt le septuor.

As with all Mallarmé's later work it is futile and meaningless to
give these lines anything approaching a literal translation but an
expanded rendering of the poem is as follows: 'The uplifted fingers

of an onyx statuette, whose twisted body symbolizes the poet's anguish, hold up in the darkness the candle-flame in which the poet, a Phœnix among men, has burned the manuscripts of his earlier unsuccessful attempts at poetry. There is no urn on the side-board in the empty room to collect the ashes of these dreams, not even a sea-shell, for this symbol of the emergence of something from nothing, this trivial empty object in which the sound of the sea can be heard, has been removed by the master of the room who has sorrowfully decided to end his life as a poet. But near to the window open to the north stands a gilt-framed mirror on which carved unicorns, in the dying light of the candle, seem to be charg-ing a water-nymph whose naked body has sunk beneath the lake-like surface of the glass. And in the emptiness of this mirror enclosed by its frame rise up the reflections of the seven stars of the constellation of the Great Bear.'

Like the poems of Baudelaire, Verlaine and Rimbaud this could be taken as a purely descriptive poem, but bearing in mind the original title, *Allegorical Sonnet about Himself*, and taking account also of Mallarmé's ideas, this empty room (a favourite image of Mallarmé's at this period) is undoubtedly symbolic of the poet's mind, and in fact it is the process of creating a void within himself which is described in the poem. Not only does he implicitly com-pare his mind to a 'chambre vide' but this empty room has been emptied of the very symbol of emptiness – an empty sea-shell. Apart from the flickering candle flame, the only thing in the sym-bolic room is a mirror, which in itself has no existence but simply reflects and underlines the emptiness. Mallarmé thus emphasizes, and indeed conveys the notion of 'le néant' throughout thirteen lines of the sonnet until, in the very last line there is the sudden and magical change as, in the empty surface of the mirror facing north through the open window, rises the symbol of 'l'infini', the huge constellation which dominates the sky beyond.

In this magnificent sonnet Mallarmé is therefore in effect saying what he had said earlier in his letter to Cazalis, that he was 'une aptitude qu'a l'univers spirituel à se voir et à se développer à travers ce qui fut moi'. But he is also giving some indication of the kind of lines along which he was working in order to create his absent world. For example, the constellation of the Great Bear is never named, nor is even the word 'star' ever used, so that in a sense it is wrong to say that at the end of the poem the constellation of the Great Bear appears in the mirror; what actually appear are seven sparkling points of light created by Mallarmé, seven stars absent, one might say, from any known sky. Furthermore, not only does Mallarmé offer the visual image of seven mysterious points of light appearing in a mirror in an empty room, but he conveys a similar impression by auditive means in that the rhyme scheme, which is an astonishing *tour de force*, is based exclusively on the two rhymes 'or' and 'ix', the one having as its primary meaning 'gold', the generally accepted symbol for the ideal world, as in 'Eldorado' and 'the golden age', and the other being the phonetic transcription in French of the letter 'x', the universally accepted symbol for the unknown. Thus not only does Mallarmé offer the visual image of a vast constellation rising out of the void, but he also conveys the same impression by auditive means thanks to this constant alternation throughout the poem of 'ix' and 'or'.

To create something from nothing in this extraordinarily complex way, to use all the resources of language, not to describe a reality which already exists outside the poem, but to create a new, hitherto non-existent reality, is a daunting task and one which Mallarmé never carried through to a successful conclusion. For thirty years, until his death in 1898, he laboured at what he called his 'Grand Oeuvre', an expression which not only means 'Great Work' but also means, in French, the philosopher's stone of the alchemists which was to turn base metal into gold. But nothing (or virtually nothing – the critics are divided on this point) of

Mallarmé's labours has come down to us, and the few poems he wrote between 1868 and 1898, totalling only about thirty, most of them sonnets, are incidental poems, or what he himself modestly called 'études en vue de mieux, comme on essaie les becs de sa plume avant de se mettre à l'œuvre' ('preliminary studies in the hope of doing something better, rather as one tries out one's pen nib before settling down to work'). Several of these poems, like *Ses Purs Ongles*, deal with his attempts to create his new reality while others deal with one particular variation on the theme of 'l'infini du néant' – that of eternal life arising out of death. Most of the latter are elegies to well-known literary figures of the day – Gautier, Edgar Poe, Baudelaire and Verlaine – and to the composer Wagner, and they follow the usual elegiac pattern of proclaiming that although the poet is dead he continues to live on in his work: 'Le splendide génie éternel n'a pas d'ombre' – 'the splendour of eternal genius cannot be dimmed'. One of these poems, however, is addressed to a friend whose wife had recently died and the final three lines are worth quoting not only because they stress the creative power of the word, which can bring the dead woman back from the grave, but also because, like the lines of *Ses Purs Ongles*, their poetic magic is such that they do in fact achieve this as the reader listens to the dead woman's plea to return from the cold graveyard to the warmth and light of the fireside and to be re-called to life simply by hearing her name murmured throughout the night:

> Ame au si clair foyer tremblante de m'asseoir,
> Pour revivre il suffit qu'à tes lèvres j'emprunte
> Le souffle de mon nom murmuré tout un soir.

Mallarmé did not therefore entirely fail in his ambition to distil something from nothing, to create life from death. But there was a period, between 1885 and 1890, when he temporarily abandoned these ambitions in favour of the less intellectual pleasures afforded by a certain Méry Laurent who had earlier been the mistress and the model of the painter Edouard Manet. He still, however, continued to write poetry, and poetry of the same kind in the sense that he still used what he called 'des mots allusifs, jamais directs' and that he still aimed at suggesting rather than describing. Just as the first line of *Ses Purs Ongles* ends with the sound 'ix' and the last line with the sound 'or', so one of his love sonnets begins with the words 'la chevelure' and ends with the word 'torche' and in between these two poles Mallarmé twists and turns his syntax so as to cram into the fourteen lines of his poem an astonishing number of words evocative of light and warmth – 'flamme', 'occident', 'diadème', 'couronne', 'foyer', 'or', 'ignition', 'feu', 'joyau', 'astres', 'feux', 'fulgurante', 'rubis' and 'écorche'. But what he thus manages to convey, by a process of repetition far more intensive than anything Baudelaire and Verlaine had ever used, is an inner feeling rather than an ideal form, which means that in the late 1880s he changed from being a transcendental Symbolist into being a human Symbolist. His purpose is to re-create in the reader, through a visual impression of the flame-like quality of Méry Laurent's flowing red hair, the warm sense of well-being and the radiant feeling of happiness he experiences in the presence of this woman who, as he mentions in the last two lines (holding back the clue to the meaning of the symbol, like Baudelaire, until the very end) sweeps away or, strictly speaking, burns away his doubts and fears and makes him feel a prince among men:

> La chevelure, vol d'une flamme, à l'extrême
> Occident de désirs pour la tout déployer,
> Se pose (je dirais mourir un diadème)
> Vers le front couronné, son ancien foyer.
>
> Mais, sans or soupirer que cette vive nue,
> L'ignition du feu toujours intérieur,
> Originellement la seule, continue
> Dans le joyau de l'oeil véridique ou rieur.

Une nudité de héros tendre diffame
Celle qui, ne mouvant astre ni feux au doigt,
Rien qu'à simplifier avec gloire la femme,
Accomplit par son chef, fulgurante, l'exploit

De semer de rubis le doute qu'elle écorche
Ainsi qu'une joyeuse et tutélaire torche.

(Her hair was once like a leaping flame, but now, as the desire to loose
these tresses finally wanes, they coil themselves, like a fading diadem,
round her head to form a crown set upon the source from which the
flame once sprang.

But there is no need now to sigh for the vivid cloud of her unbound
hair; for the light of the inner flame of love, of which her hair was
once the only sign, continues to shine in the sparkle of her frank and
laughing eyes.

A lover's sensual gesture would be an insult to this woman who,
although her fingers, with their rings and jewels, no longer move to
loosen her hair, is still the glorious essence of womanhood, with a
radiance about her which enables her to accomplish the feat of acting
upon the poet like a joyful and protective flame, dispelling all his
doubts and replacing them with the feeling that he is the most fortu-
nate of men.)

It must be confessed that, in an attempt to simplify the meaning,
a number of full-stops and commas have been inserted in the
French version that are absent from the original. Many critics may
well disagree with the punctuation suggested, since it presumes a
certain interpretation that they may not share, and other critics may
well deplore any additions whatever of this kind, since Mallarmé
deliberately omitted virtually all punctuation from his later poems,
no doubt because he felt that it was an inadequate system to reflect
all the subtleties and complexities of his syntax.

Merely to abandon punctuation, however, was a negative answer
to the problem of how to deal with an increasingly rich and involved means of expression, and in 1897, the year before his death,

Mallarmé adopted a much more positive solution in a uniquely revolutionary work whose main clause, 'Un coup de dés jamais n'abolira le hasard', is printed in large capitals with the words irregularly spaced over some twenty pages. A number of subordinate clauses, some in smaller capitals, some in ordinary lettering and some in italics, are interspersed among the words of the main clause. The pages are treated as double pages so that sentences flow across from the left-hand page to the right-hand page. In devising this system Mallarmé was clearly breaking away from the restraints of conventional forms of expression more than any of his fellow Symbolist poets. The use of different lettering enabled him to convey by visual means the importance of the main clause and to indicate the various subordinate clauses far more clearly than by the use of punctuation. But above all perhaps, by using the larger area of the double page and by distributing a relatively small number of words across the pages in an irregular pattern, he introduced a pictorial element into poetry. Much of the imagery of *Un Coup de Dés* is concerned with the sea and the sky and there is no doubt that the words sometimes set in isolation on the double page, like black stars in a white sky, and the lines of print trailing across the paper, like the negative of a photograph of the wake of a ship, are intended to reinforce this imagery, much as the sounds 'ix' and 'or' are intended to complement the visual effects in *Ses Purs Ongles*. There is indeed a close relationship between these two works, although the optimism implicit in the constellation rising triumphantly out of the empty room has given way to a calm resignation implicit in a similar constellation quietly presiding over a catastrophic shipwreck. This is the wreck of Mallarmé's ambition to transform the ideal into reality, but he finds consolation in the thought that even if he had published his *Grand Oeuvre*, it might nevertheless have sunk into oblivion; to seize the chance of publication, as many a poet knows, still leaves open the chance that what one publishes may remain unread – 'un coup de dés jamais n'abolira le hasard'. He finds further consolation, however, in the thought that, even if one does not publish, one's ideas nevertheless have an equal chance of being disseminated by other means – 'toute pensée émet un coup de dés' is the modest conclusion, printed in suitably modest lettering, of this extraordinarily original and complex work, the final passage of which runs as follows:

UNE CONSTELLATION

froide d'oubli et de désuétude
pas tant
qu'elle n'énumère
sur quelque surface vacante et supérieure
le heurt successif
sidéralement
d'un compte total en formation

veillant
doutant
roulant
brillant et méditant

avant de s'arrêter
à quelque point dernier qui le sacre

Toute Pensée émet un Coup de Dés

6

Valéry's return to reality

Mallarmé's ideas did indeed have an effect out of all proportion to the small volume of work he produced. He exercised his influence in particular through his celebrated 'mardis', the Tuesday evening meetings which were attended not only by many of the established authors of the day but also by younger writers, among whom Paul Valéry shared that sense of dissatisfaction with reality common to all the Symbolist poets. Partly, however, through the belief that Mallarmé had gone as far as was possible along the road towards creating an 'ideal' poetry, and partly because his own early verse tended to be of an emotional rather than an intellectual nature, Valéry virtually abandoned poetry in 1892 at the age of twenty-one and turned his attention instead to other ways of exploring the world of ideas. He was particularly fascinated by philosophy, mathematics and physics, and although he never acquired the highly specialized knowledge in these subjects that would have enabled him to make a contribution to new views on, for example, the structure of the universe, he clearly revealed his admiration for this kind of intellectual activity in his *Introduction à la Méthode de Léonard de Vinci* in 1895 where he attributed to the universal genius of the Italian Renaissance the capacity for methodically tracing the hidden relationships between various fields of knowledge. Similarly the character of M. Teste, which Valéry created in 1894 and whose name derives from the French word for 'head', is a man of powerful intellect, who, in *La Soirée avec M. Teste*, succeeds in discovering new laws that govern the working of the human mind and who is totally divorced from the realities of everyday life.

Though it would perhaps be wrong to equate Valéry entirely with M. Teste, there is no doubt that he too remained extraordinarily detached from life for some twenty years, able to pursue his intellectual meditations undisturbed thanks to the generosity of a wealthy business-man who, in 1900, offered him a sinecure as his private secretary, a post which he retained until the death of his patron in 1922. Valéry's state of mind at this time is perhaps best described in the early verses of his celebrated poem *Le Cimetière Marin*, first published in 1920, where he recollects the sense of hypnotic tranquillity he had experienced in the contemplation of eternity and infinity into which he had felt absorbed:

> Comme le fruit se fond en jouissance,
> Comme en délice il change son absence
> Dans une bouche où sa forme se meurt,
> Je hume ici ma future fumée.

> (As the fruit melts into enjoyment,
> As it is absorbed and changed into pleasure
> In the mouth where it ceases to exist,
> So I have here a foretaste of the dust and
> ashes I will become.)

Yet both M. Teste and his creator found that the emotional side of life, the contact with reality and with the world of the senses, could not be permanently abandoned or suppressed. In a later part of the Teste cycle of nine short prose works, Mme Emilie Teste writes of her husband:

Quand il me revient de la profondeur, il a l'air de me découvrir comme une terre nouvelle! . . . Il me saisit aveuglément dans ses bras, comme si j'étais un rocher de vie et de présence réelle où ce grand génie incommunicable se heurterait, toucherait, s'accrocherait, après tant d'inhumains silences monstreux.

(When he returns to me from the depths, he seems to discover me as if I were a new world! . . . He takes me blindly in his arms as if I were a rock of life and of present reality which this great and lonely genius could come up against, and touch and cling on to, after so strange and inhuman a period of silence.)

Similarly Valéry, after his long years of introspection, 'returned from the depths' and experienced a renewed desire to make fresh contact with the world of the senses in about 1912 when he was persuaded to gather together some of his early verse with a view to publishing a volume of poetry, which appeared in 1920 under the title of *Album de Vers Anciens*. Though he began to revise these lines written twenty years before with a feeling of reluctance and even hostility towards something he now regarded as completely alien to him, he was gradually recaptured by the pleasure of writing poetry and by the renewed impact that the world of sensual reality had on him. It is this that forms the fundamental theme of the poem, at first intended to be of no more than thirty or forty lines, which he began to write in 1912 to add to his early verse and which grew, as he worked on it for the next four or five years, to more than five hundred lines. The title of this work, *La Jeune Parque*, refers to Clotho, the youngest of the three fates whose task it is to spin the thread of life and it is she whose thoughts and feelings are explored in the poem. Her awakening to the realization that within her 'une secrète soeur brûle' can reasonably be equated initially, whatever the wider implications of this complex and difficult poem may be, with Valéry's own awakening to the realization that within him a sensitive poet still existed; the temptations and hesitations she experiences probably reflect Valéry's own uncertainties during these years when he was re-examining his own position; and her willingness, at the end of the poem, to face the wind, the sea and the sun which Valéry so vividly remembered from his younger days spent in the port of Sète on the Mediterranean coast, no doubt has its equivalent in his decision to abandon the exclusively intellectual ambitions of M. Teste and to make place as well for the world of the senses.

A similar kind of theme recurs in *Le Cimetière Marin* where the famous final cry in the last verse: 'Le vent se lève! . . . il faut tenter de vivre!', as the poet finds renewed vitality in the exhilarating feel of the breeze blowing over the tombs in the cemetery by the sea which forms the setting of the poem, could well belong to *La Jeune Parque* whose heroine also stands facing the keen wind blowing in from the sea:

> L'être contre le vent, dans le plus vif de l'air
> Recevant au visage un appel de la mer.

Otherwise, however, the two poems are rather different and might be said to reach the same conclusion from opposite directions in that the one deals evocatively with the symbolic heroine's slow awakening to the knowledge of the temptations of life to which she finally and willingly submits, while the other analyses the way in which Valéry had succumbed to the opposite temptation of contemplating eternity and waiting for death until the moment of his final revolt against inaction:

> Brisez, mon corps, cette forme pensive!
> Buvez, mon sein, la naissance du vent!
> Une fraîcheur, de la mer exhalée
> Me rend mon âme . . . O puissance salée!
> Courons à l'onde en rejaillir vivant!
>
> (Let my body break the bonds of thought.
> Let me breathe in the wind that is rising.
> A freshening breeze blowing in from the sea
> Gives me back my soul. Let me plunge into the waves
> And rise out of them a living being once more.)

Valéry has, therefore, not unlike Mallarmé in the late 1880s, returned to reality and has recognized that the mind cannot remain turned in on itself but must accept the importance of the world of the senses. But whereas Mallarmé, to put it in its simplest terms, forsook his goal of constructing an ideal world through the medium of his poetry in favour of writing poems in celebration of Méry Laurent, Valéry's curiously detached mind was fascinated not by reality itself, but by the fact of his return to reality. It is not so much, therefore, the renewed impact that the sensual world had on him from 1912 onwards as his conscious awareness of this renewed impact that gives Valéry's later poetry its unique quality. His intellectual self was able to stand back and observe his sensual self at work, joining forces with it on occasions so as to urge it forward or hold it in check or divert it into certain channels. In various ways all the poems in *Charmes* which Valéry wrote between 1917 and 1922 are concerned with this complex problem of the relationship between mind and body and with the contribution that both must make to the creative process. In a sense the entire volume is a kind of 'art poétique' in that, although the poems are, of course, poems in their own right – and some of them are among the finest in French literature – they are also poems about writing poetry.

Yet, fascinated though he was by his new-found conviction that contact with the world of the senses is necessary for the poet to exercise his function as a creative artist and that the stimulus thus provided must then be controlled and guided by the poet's mind, Valéry, like Mallarmé, did not produce any later *Grand Oeuvre* putting his principles into practice and demonstrating how the alliance of the mind and the senses could yield fruitful results. Though he still had over twenty years to live after the appearance of *Charmes* in 1922, he published no more poetry and the prose works with which he increasingly busied himself tend to be either comparatively light-weight comment and criticism or to embroider on the fundamental theme of *Charmes* – the need for a reconciliation between thought and action. One of his last works, two unfinished plays on the theme of Dr Faustus which Valéry sketched out rapidly in 1940, reveal that his thoughts still ran along the same lines. Just as M. Teste had emerged from his meditations to cling to his wife as if to 'un rocher de vie et de présence réelle', so Valéry's Faustus declares that:

> Le moindre regard, la moindre sensation, les moindres actes et fonctions de la vie me deviennent de la même dignité que les desseins et les voix intérieures de ma pensée . . . C'est un état suprême, où tout se résume en vivre.

> The merest glance, the slightest sensation, the most fleeting act and activity in my outward life acquire the same dignity as the designs and dictates of my inward thoughts . . . This is the supreme state in which to be, where everything is summed up in the words: to live.

In terms of the content of his work, therefore, Valéry cannot properly be described as either a human symbolist or a transcendental symbolist. He does not use reality to convey his own feelings and, except in those lines of *Le Cimetière Marin* recalling his long period of meditation, he does not look beyond reality to another world. As far as the form of his work is concerned, however, he is very much a descendant of Baudelaire and Mallarmé. To suggest rather than to describe is as much his aim as it is that of the earlier Symbolist poets, and like them he often leaves the meaning of his images implicit rather than explicit. A notable example is the opening image in *Le Cimetière Marin* of a roof on which doves are perched and which can be glimpsed through the pine trees and the tombs of the cemetery at Sète:

> Ce toit tranquille, où marchent des colombes,
> Entre les pins palpite, entre les tombes.

Although the adjective 'tranquille' and the verb 'palpiter' give a hint of the meaning, it is only in the following line that one realizes that this 'roof' is in fact the vast expanse of the sea, shimmering in the fierce light of noon with the sun at its zenith:

> Midi le juste y compose de feux
> La mer, la mer, toujours recommencée,

and not until the very last line of this fairly long poem of twenty-four verses is the image of the doves deciphered when one learns that these were in fact the jibsails of boats dipping down towards the water in a pecking motion similar to that of birds on a roof:

> Ce toit tranquille où picoraient des focs.

The sonnet *L'Abeille* is an equally notable example. Taken at its face value it is simply a poem about a woman asking to be stung by a bee, although even the most obtuse reader would no doubt recognize the erotic overtones of this image. But ought one to look further still and perceive a third plane of meaning concerned with the problem of the creative process and the necessity for the poet to turn towards the world of the senses? Only a reference in the last three lines, to the senses being awakened by the tiny golden sting without which love dies or remains dormant suggests that, as in so so many of Valéry's poems, a deeper meaning of this kind may be intended:

> Soit donc mon sens illuminé
> Par cette infime alerte d'or
> Sans qui l'Amour meurt ou s'endort.

Almost all the poems in *Charmes* are in fact extended metaphors of this kind – an oarsman rowing doggedly upstream in *Le Rameur*, for example, or a tree secretly and silently growing in *Palme*, or a fruit slowly ripening in *Les Grenades* – and there is little or no indication in the poems themselves that what they are really concerned with is the creative power of both the conscious and the unconscious mind and the contribution that both must make to the poet's work.

Not only is Valéry a Symbolist in that he thus leaves his symbols virtually unexplained, he also belongs to the Symbolists in that he is one of the most musical of poets. His definition of poetry as 'cette hésitation prolongée entre le son et le sens' has been mentioned in an earlier chapter and it is this that makes Valéry's poems almost impossible to translate since they are made up of lines of music as well as of lines of words. 'Je hume ici ma future fumée' from *Le Cimetière Marin* is one of the best-known examples of these lines which are so characteristic of Valéry, where the sound is almost more important than the sense. It is a similarly audacious use of assonance and alliteration which matters as much as, and perhaps even more than the meaning in these opening lines from *L'Abeille*:

> Quelle, et si fine, et si mortelle,
> Que soit ta pointe, blonde abeille,
> Je n'ai, sur ma tendre corbeille
> Jeté qu'un songe de dentelle,

or in these lines describing, or rather evoking, a sleeping girl:

> Souffle, songes, silence, invincible accalmie,
> Tu triomphes, ô paix plus puissante qu'un pleur,
> Quand de ce plein sommeil l'onde grave et l'ampleur
> Conspirent sur le sein d'une telle ennemie.
>
> Dormeuse, amas doré d'ombres et d'abandons . . .

Yet these are no more than traditional poetic practices pushed to extreme limits by the conscious artistry that Valéry, following in the footsteps of Mallarmé in this respect, brought to bear in the sphere of form as well as content. As regards versification Valéry is in fact a fundamentally conventional poet who made less attempt to break its 'cruel bonds' than any of his predecessors. There is nothing in his work comparable to the startling originality of Mallarmé's *Un Coup de Dés* or of Rimbaud's *Illuminations* and by thus becoming reconciled to traditional means of poetic expression, just as he had become reconciled to reality, Valéry may be said, despite the suggestive rather than the descriptive nature of his poetry with its extraordinary musicality, to mark the end of Symbolism.

7

The repercussions of Symbolism

Symbolism, as the term has so far been understood in this study, is limited to a small number of outstanding French poets from about 1850 to about 1920 all of whom had a number of aims in common. But certain particular aspects of Symbolism, to the exclusion of other aspects, were taken up by lesser poets and by writers in other fields and in other countries so that Symbolism had extensive repercussions in one way or another, although the writers concerned may perhaps more properly be said to have been influenced by Symbolism rather than to have been true Symbolists according to all the criteria that have been indicated in the preceding pages.

The technical innovations of Symbolism, for example, held a particular fascination for authors such as Gustave Kahn, the great advocate of the use of free verse in the closing years of the nineteenth century in France, and René Ghil, founder of the 'école instrumentiste', who pushed to extremes the Symbolists' ideas on musicality and on the importance of the sheer sound of words. Others were attracted more by the anti-reality side of Symbolism, such as Jules Laforgue who, in the half-dozen years before his death in 1887 at the early age of twenty-seven, looked sardonically at human life, barely concealing his despair at man's inability to bring about any change. Others again, influenced by the pessimistic and morbid nature of the later poems in Baudelaire's *Fleurs du Mal*, turned away from reality only to plunge into a horrifying nightmare world. This is the case with Isidore Ducasse, better known under his pseudonym of Lautréamont, who published as early as 1868 and 1869 his *Chants de Maldoror*, a long unfinished prose poem where the unreality of the content is matched by the originality of the form.

The largest and most important category of writers, however, turned away from reality with an optimistic attitude and set about creating their ideal world. The theatre, in particular, seemed to lend itself to this idealist side of Symbolism. Mallarmé, at an early stage in his career in about 1865 had attempted two unusual verse dramas, *L'Après-midi d'un Faune* and *Hérodiade*, both of which are entirely divorced from reality and create a strange atmosphere of mystery and hallucination, while at the same time Wagner was re-creating in his operas the mysterious world of medieval legend. Wagner's enormous influence in France in the last quarter of the nineteenth century, particularly with the founding, in 1885, of the *Revue Wagnérienne*, allied to that of Mallarmé, did much to encourage dramatists to abandon realism in the theatre and to create in their plays a sense of mystery, using poetic language and unrealistic settings. Three of the most notable of these dramatists were Villiers de l'Isle Adam, with his plays *Elën*, *Morgane* and *Axël*, whose titles alone suffice to indicate their strong Wagnerian influence, Maurice Maeterlinck, with such plays as *La Princesse Maleine*, *Les Aveugles* and *Pelléas et Mélisande* which, as one critic has put it, 'portray essentially passive characters subject to the overpowering pressures of hidden, mysterious forces', and Paul Claudel, most of whose plays were written in the early years of the twentieth century although it was not until the 1940s that his epic dramas such as *Partage de Midi* and *Le Soulier de Satin*, concerned with the great Christian issues of sin and redemption, were finally staged.

The idealist side of Symbolism can be discerned in the novel as well as in the theatre. Villiers de l'Isle Adam, for example, in *L'Eve future*, looked forward to a new paradise, much as he had done in his play *Axël* that has been mentioned above, and the hero of J. K. Huysmans's novel *A Rebours*, published in 1884, lives in an exotic artificial world of jewels and perfumes not unlike the one of which Baudelaire had dreamed. But Huysmans was converted to Catholicism in the closing years of the century and his longing for another world took a course parallel to that taken by Claudel in works such as *La Cathédrale*, a fervent evocation of Chartres cathedral and of the joys of a life devoted to the service of Christianity.

The greatest novelist in whom the influence of Symbolism can be detected, and in its purest form (although the concept of a Symbolist novel is not one which has ever made any great headway among literary historians), is, however, Marcel Proust who, from 1913 to 1922, wrote his long and basically autobiographical novel, *A la Recherche du Temps Perdu* which, as the title suggests, aims at penetrating behind reality in search of an ideal world. Proust, more than anyone, achieves that stereoscopic effect mentioned in the first chapter of this study, and true reality for him springs from a fusion of the present and the past. Just as Jeanne Duval's hair awakens in Baudelaire memories of his trip to the tropics and just as this fusion of a past memory with present reality creates for him 'l'oasis où je rêve', so Proust tastes the little cake called a 'madeleine' he had tasted as a child and all the memories of his early days in Illiers, the small market town near Chartres which he calls Combray in his novel, come flooding back to him, purified and crystallized by the passage of time; or he steps on an uneven paving stone, similar to one he had stepped on in Venice many years before, and those forgotten and even unnoticed days suddenly come to life for him. 'Je dis: une fleur!', Mallarmé had said, 'et, hors de l'oubli où ma voix relègue aucun contour . . . se lève . . . l'absente de tous bouquets'; similarly, from behind the vast panorama of Parisian society that Proust depicts in *A la Recherche du Temps Perdu* emerges a new and fascinating world peopled by men situated, as the final words of the novel put it, not in space but in time.

The desire to escape from reality was, however, already taking another form during the years when Proust was slowly and elaborately composing *A la Recherche du Temps Perdu*. A number of writers led by André Breton had perceived within Symbolism a conflict between the impatient genius of Arthur Rimbaud, advocating that the poet should allow his thoughts to develop uncontrolled, and the patient genius of Mallarmé and his disciple Valéry, giving a vitally important rôle to the controlling power of the intellect over inspiration. Breton and his followers preferred Rimbaud's approach, which had also been that of Lautréamont, and these two Symbolists became the fountainheads of the Surrealist movement which, from about 1920, became the new rallying point for those who wished to penetrate beyond reality. But Surrealism is clearly distinguishable from Symbolism not only by the emphasis it lays on means rather than ends, on the use of irrational methods rather than on the nature of the super-reality thus attained, but also by its attachment to painting instead of music as having particularly close links with literature, since painting clearly lends itself far more readily to the practice of the kind of principles on which Surrealism was based.

While Symbolism was thus being modified and transformed within the frontiers of its country of origin, it was making its impact outside France. Among English writers, or, to be more accurate, writers in English, the idealist side of Symbolism made a particular appeal to W. B. Yeats who, from his early twenties was interested in the occult and in the world of Irish legend. Although his knowledge of French was slight, he acknowledged his debt to Villiers de l'Isle Adam's *Axël* and he must have known of the other French Symbolists through his friend Arthur Symons whose book, *The Symbolist Movement in Literature*, published in 1899, names Yeats as their principal heir. Yeats's imagery, of course, whether it belongs to his world of Celtic twilight or to the complex philosophical system he elaborated as a result of his interest in the occult, is very much of his own devising, but *Sailing to Byzantium*, for example, can nevertheless be said to belong to the same kind of poetry as Baudelaire's *Le Voyage*, Rimbaud's *Le Bateau Ivre*, and Mallarmé's *Un Coup de Dés* in that all these works, through an accumulation of powerful images, create an impression of the spiritual goal each poet is seeking even when the origin and meaning of the symbols used is not fully understood.

On the other hand the Imagist group of English and American poets, led by T. E. Hulme and Ezra Pound, who invented the term in 1912, were attracted by the tendency of Baudelaire and Laforgue in particular to dwell on the grimmer aspects of reality. The images of the Imagists are not, therefore, symbols in the sense that this term has been defined in the first chapter of the present study, but simply metaphors and similes which were made deliberately original and startling so as to shock the reader. But although the Imagists might therefore be said to be almost anti-Symbolist in that they are too concerned with the outward, concrete image to the neglect of any abstract idea or emotion lying behind it, this is not true of one of their number, T. S. Eliot, who joined the group in 1915 but who soon came to use such images as 'the yellow fog that rubs its back upon the window panes' and 'the burnt-out ends of smoky days' not simply for the sake of making his descriptions more powerful, but so as to convey and create a mood, in the manner of Baudelaire. One might in fact say of Eliot what he himself said of Baudelaire – that his importance lay 'not merely in the use of the imagery of the sordid life of a great metropolis, but in the elevation of such imagery to the first intensity – presenting it as it is and yet making it represent something much more than itself'. Like Baudelaire too, or like the later Baudelaire, he is not only a human Symbolist who evokes the emotion behind the image, he is also a transcendental Symbolist of a pessimistic bent who sees life for the most part as a waste land, a 'correspondance de l'enfer' rather than a 'correspondance du ciel'. But the positive side of transcendental Symbolism, the optimistic belief in the creation of an ideal world through the medium of poetry, seems to have made no appeal to Eliot and it may be for this reason that, as he once said to Francis Scarfe (see the latter's essay in Graham Martin's *Eliot in Perspective*), he was 'not particularly interested in Rimbaud' and never appears to have appreciated the achievement of Mallarmé. He found himself much nearer in spirit to Baudelaire, once the latter had sunk from 'l'idéal' to 'le spleen', and just as Baudelaire, in the last years of his life after the second edition of *Les Fleurs du Mal* in 1861, seemed to be moving more and more towards a religious rather than a poetic solution to his despondency at the world around him, so Eliot, after his adoption of Anglo-Catholicism in 1927, seems to have found in Christianity a counter to his pessimism.

But if Eliot followed the example of Baudelaire in dwelling on the sordid side of life as the 'objective correlative' of his pessimism, it was the example of a far less important poet, Jules Laforgue, vastly overrated by Eliot and his fellow Imagists, which led him to express this view of life in a form very different from Baudelaire's measured alexandrines and rhetorical style. For not only was Laforgue's pessimism tinged with a sardonic note, as has been mentioned above, which made a particular appeal to Eliot, but he also adopted Gustave Kahn's free verse techniques which were an eminently suitable vehicle for sudden changes of tone, and Eliot transposed these techniques into English with telling effect.

German literature, as well as English literature, was influenced by French Symbolism and it is the two outstanding poets of the early part of the twentieth century, Rainer Maria Rilke and Stefan George, in whom this influence can most clearly be seen. Rilke acknowledged the debt he owed to Paul Valéry, whose *Cimetière marin* he translated and whose influence left its mark in particular on his final and finest works, published in 1923, the *Duino Elegies* and the *Sonnets to Orpheus*. But, more generally, Rilke is cast very much in the Symbolist mould by virtue of his constant search for a greater reality behind and beyond the surface of experience and by virtue of his use, in the *Elegies*, of *vers libre*, well fitted, as C. M. Bowra puts it, 'to express the subtle and sinuous movements of a soul communing with itself'. George too was dedicated to the pursuit of a spiritual life and was deeply impressed by Mallarmé whom he met during the time he spent in Paris in the last decade of the nineteenth century. But his life ran curiously parallel to that of Verlaine rather than Mallarmé in his obsession with an almost Rimbaud-like figure, Maximin, whom he idolized and idealized as the symbol of a new heroic age, the coming of which he heralded in such quasi-mystical poetry as *The Seventh Ring* published in 1907, some three years after the premature death of its hero.

The influence of Symbolism extended beyond Germany to Russia where a number of writers in the 1890s and in the early years of the twentieth century enthusiastically adopted the ideas of the French Symbolists. Some leaned towards human Symbolism, such as Bryusov who wrote in 1894 that 'the Symbolist tries to arouse in the reader by the melody of his verse a particular mood', while others were transcendental Symbolists, such as Volynsky who wrote in 1900 that 'Symbolism is the fusion of the phenomenal and divine worlds in artistic representation' and Bely who stated in 1906 that 'a symbol is the integument of a Platonic Idea' (see J. West's *Russian Symbolism*).

To discuss in greater detail these distant repercussions of French Symbolism would, however, be outside the scope of this short study and the limited competence of its author. Suffice it to say that if poetry in France in the last half of the nineteenth century had not led the way in the use of outward symbols to convey unexplained emotions and ideas, and if it had not shaken off, more vigorously than Romanticism had done half a century earlier, all the old conventions as regards literary forms, then later poets, playwrights and novelists in other countries might have lacked the courage and the confidence to open up their new paths. It may well be in fact that the effects of Symbolism have not yet ceased to reverberate and that the strangely real yet unreal world of so many works of literature written at the present day, the way in which they try to create an emotional state rather than to put across an intellectual message, and the unconventional forms which they so often take will be seen, in future years, to be indebted in no small measure to the Symbolist poetry of late-nineteenth-century France.

Select Bibliography

ADAM, ANTOINE, *Verlaine*, Paris, 1965 (latest edition).
A competent study in the 'Connaissance des Lettres' series
translated into English under the title *The Art of Paul Verlaine*,
published by New York University Press, 1963.

AUSTIN, L. J., *L'univers poétique de Baudelaire*, Paris, 1956.
A sound study of *Les Fleurs du Mal* in which the author tried to
launch the rather confusing terms 'symbolisme' and 'symbolique' for what we have called 'human symbolism' and 'transcendental symbolism'.

BALAKIAN, ANNA, *The Symbolist Movement*, New York, 1967.
The word 'movement' in the title is the operative one, since the
author starts with Swedenborg and ends with Samuel Beckett,
though a large part of the book is devoted to Baudelaire, Verlaine and Mallarmé.

BATTERBY, K. A. J., *Rilke and France*, London, 1966.
Particular attention is paid to the influence of Baudelaire and
Valéry on Rilke.

BLOCK, HASKELL M., *Mallarmé and the Symbolist Drama*,
Detroit, 1963.
A short study of Mallarmé's dramatic theory and practice in re-
lation to the theatre in the last two decades of the nineteenth
century.

BONNEFOY, Y., *Rimbaud par lui-même*, Paris, 1961.
A study of one poet by another.

BORNECQUE, J. H., *Verlaine par lui-même*, Paris, 1966.
As the title implies, this volume, like others in the series, tries to stick as closely as possible to material from the poet's own pen.

BOWRA, C. M., *The Heritage of Symbolism*, London, 1943.
There is a useful introductory essay on Symbolism, but the rest of the book, as the title implies, is devoted to essays on five writers of the succeeding generation – Valéry, Rilke, George, Blok and Yeats.

CHADWICK, C., *Etudes sur Rimbaud*, Paris, 1960.
A collection of ten essays on various aspects of Rimbaud's life and work.

CHADWICK, C., *Mallarmé, sa pensée dans sa poésie*, Paris, 1962.
This short study, as the title implies, aims at tracing the development of Mallarmé's thought in his poetry.

CHARPIER, J., *Essai sur Paul Valéry*, Paris, 1956.
This is one of the useful 'Poètes d'aujourd'hui' series.

CHIARI, J., *Symbolisme, from Poe to Mallarmé*, London, 1956.
These are virtually two separate essays, one on Symbolism, taken in a wide and woolly sense, and the other on the influence of Poe on Mallarmé.

CORNELL, KENNETH, *The Symbolist Movement*, New Haven, Conn., 1951.
The title might more properly have been *The Symbolist Period*, since the book is a year by year account of the period from 1885 to 1900 in France.

CORNELL, KENNETH, *The Post-Symbolist Period*, New Haven, Conn., 1958.
This sequel to *The Symbolist Movement*, with a more fitting title, follows a similar pattern in tracing French poetic currents from 1900 to 1920.

DANIELS, MAY, *The French Drama of the Unspoken*, Edinburgh, 1953.

The early chapters are devoted to a study of the French theatre after 1870 and of Maeterlinck.

DAVIES, G., *Les Tombeaux de Mallarmé*, Paris, 1950, *Vers une explication rationelle du 'Coup de Dés'*, Paris, 1953, *Mallarmé et le drame solaire*, Paris, 1959, *Les Noces d'Hérodiade*, Paris, 1959.

In these four volumes a leading Mallarmé scholar has made a massive contribution to the elucidating of much of Mallarmé's best poetry.

DONCHIN, G., *The Influence of French Symbolism on Russian Poetry*, The Hague, 1958.

A thorough and well-documented study of this subject.

ETIEMBLE, R., *Le Mythe de Rimbaud*, Paris, 1952–61.

This is a vast study in four volumes of which the final one seems unlikely to appear. Vol. I, *La Genèse du Mythe* is a huge bibliography listing the thousands of books and articles that built up, and are still building up, the Rimbaud legend. Vol. II, *La Structure du Mythe* outlines briefly the various theories that have been advanced to 'explain' Rimbaud – 'Rimbaud the Child', 'Rimbaud the Seer', 'Rimbaud the Communist', etc.

FAIRLIE, ALISON, *Les Fleurs du Mal*, London, 1960.

A short but useful study in a series published by Edward Arnold aimed at offering a sound introduction to well-known works.

FROHOCK, W. M., *Rimbaud's Poetic Practice*, Oxford, 1963.

One of the best recent studies of Rimbaud.

HACKETT, C. A., *Rimbaud l'enfant*, Paris, 1948.

A development of an earlier work, *Le Lyrisme de Rimbaud* (1938) by the same author who has also written a useful

introduction to Rimbaud in a series called 'Studies in Euro-
pean Literature and Thought' published by Bowes and Bowes in
1957, and an interesting volume of essays *Autour de Rimbaud*,
Paris, 1968.

KNOWLES, DOROTHY, *La réaction idéaliste au théâtre*, Paris,
1934.
A panorama of Symbolism and its aftermath in the French
theatre.

LAWLER, J. R., *Lecture de Valéry, une étude de 'Charmes'*, Paris,
1963.
A series of 'explications de texte' of each of the twenty-one
poems of *Charmes*.

LEHMANN, A. G., *The Symbolist Aesthetic in France 1885–1895*,
Oxford, 1950 (second edition 1968).
A wide-ranging study that emphasizes and perhaps over-
emphasizes the complexities of symbolism concluding that 'the
terms "literary symbol" and "symbolist" are terms which, introduced and fortified by a series of mischances, should never have
been allowed to remain in usage'.

LEMAITRE, H., *La Poésie depuis Baudelaire*, Paris, 1965.
This useful book consists of three sections – a history of French
poetry since Baudelaire; an 'anthologie théorique' made up of
statements about poetry by the poets of the time; and an 'anthologie poétique' giving examples of their work.

LETHÈVE, J., *Impressionistes et Symbolistes devant la Presse*,
Paris, 1959.
The title is self-explanatory and the second half contains some
interesting material relative to the battles which raged round
Symbolism in French newspapers and magazines in the late
nineteenth century.

MACKAY, AGNES, *The Universal Self, a Study of Paul Valéry*, London, 1961.
As the title implies, this is a general study of Valéry.

MARTIN, G., *Eliot in Perspective*, London, 1970.
A symposium containing, among essays by various authors on various aspects of Eliot, a study by F. Scarfe entitled 'Eliot and nineteenth-century French poetry'.

MARTINO, P., *Parnasse et Symbolisme*, Paris, 1967 (latest edition).
This standard introduction has run through many editions since it was first published in 1925, but it still serves a useful purpose.

MARTINO, P., *Verlaine*, Paris, 1951 (latest edition).
The first of the few studies there are of the poet rather than the man.

MAURON, CH., *Mallarmé par lui-même*, Paris, 1964.
A useful introduction to Mallarmé.

MICHAUD, G., *Message Poétique du Symbolisme* (3 vols.), Paris, 1947.
This is the definitive 600-page thesis on the Symbolist movement in all its ramifications and is complemented by a fourth volume, *La Doctrine Symboliste, Documents*.

MICHAUD, G., *Mallarmé*, Paris, 1953.
This is one of the best of the 'Connaissance des Lettres' series and one of the best studies of Mallarmé's life and work. It was translated into English and published by New York University Press in 1965.

MONDOR, H., *Vie de Mallarmé*, 1942.
This is the standard biography of Mallarmé.

NOULET, E., *Dix poèmes de Stéphane Mallarmé*, Paris, 1948 and *Vingt poèmes de Stéphane Mallarmé*, Paris, 1967.

As the titles imply these two volumes attempt to decipher specific poems by Mallarmé.

PETITFILS, P. and MATARASSO, H., *Vie de Rimbaud*, Paris, 1962.
The most recent biography of Rimbaud.

PINTO, V. DE S., *Crisis in English Poetry, 1880–1940*, London, 1961.
The chapters on Yeats and Eliot are particularly relevant to Symbolism.

POMMIER, JEAN, *La Mystique de Baudelaire*, Paris, 1932.
This long and penetrating 'explication de texte' of the sonnet *Correspondances* shows how it stands at the very centre of Baudelaire's poetry.

RAITT, A. W., *Villiers de L'Isle Adam et le mouvement symboliste*, Paris, 1965.
The author adopts what he calls an empirical standpoint and describes as Symbolists 'all those writers who are generally considered, rightly or wrongly, to belong to the movement'. Baudelaire, Poe, Wagner, Mallarmé and Verlaine are among those whose relationship with Villiers de L'Isle Adam is considered.

RAYMOND, M., *De Baudelaire au Surréalisme*, Paris, 1952.
The introduction is devoted to Baudelaire, Verlaine, Mallarmé and Rimbaud, while the later fortunes and misfortunes of Symbolism are examined in the opening chapters, including essays on Valéry and Claudel.

ROBICHEZ, JACQUES, *Le Symbolisme au théâtre*, Paris, 1957.
The subtitle *Lugné Poe et les debuts de 'L'Oeuvre'* defines more precisely this study of one of the leading actors of the last years of the nineteenth century and of the theatre he founded.

RUFF, M. A., *Baudelaire*, Paris, 1955.

A short but sound introduction in the 'Connaissance des Lettres' series published by Hatier.

RUFF, M. A., *Rimbaud*, Paris, 1968.
One of the latest in the 'Connaissance des Lettres' series.

SCHMIDT, A. M., *La Littérature Symboliste*, Paris, 1955.
This useful introduction in 'Que sais-je' series first published in 1942, tends to lay perhaps too much emphasis on the minor symbolist poets and too little emphasis on the major figures who are treated as 'précurseurs'.

STARKIE, ENID, *Baudelaire*, London, 1957.
An essentially biographical approach to an essentially autobiographical poet.

STARKIE, ENID, *Rimbaud*, London, 1961.
The third revised edition of the standard biography of Rimbaud in English.

STARKIE, ENID, *From Gautier to Eliot*, London, 1960.
The subtitle, *The Influence of France on English Literature, 1851–1939*, defines the subject rather more closely.

SYMONS, ARTHUR, *The Symbolist Movement in Literature*, London, 1899.
One of the earliest studies of Symbolism by an English admirer of the movement. In a short introductory essay, Symons shows that he is concerned only with 'transcendental Symbolism' and he then writes essays on eight authors to whom 'the visible world is no longer a reality and the unseen world no longer a dream' – Nerval, Villiers de l'Isle Adam, Rimbaud, Verlaine, Laforgue, Mallarmé, Huysmans and Maeterlinck.

TAUPIN, R., *L'Influence du Symbolisme français sur la poésie américaine*, Paris, 1929.

A long and interesting chapter on T. S. Eliot is no doubt the most important part of this book.

THOMSON, A. W., *Valéry*, Edinburgh, 1963.
This compact but useful volume is one of the 'Writers and Critics' series, published by Oliver and Boyd.

TURNELL, MARTIN, *Baudelaire*, London, 1953.
A readable general study of Baudelaire's poetry.

UNTERECKER, J., *Yeats, a Collection of Critical Essays*, New York, 1963.
Among these essays one by W. Y. Tindall on 'The Symbolism of W. B. Yeats' emphasizes that Yeats' debt to French Symbolism was slight and that his symbolism is very much of his own devising.

WALZER, P. O., *Essai sur Stephane Mallarmé*, Paris, 1963.
Another good introduction to Mallarmé.

WALZER, P. O., *La Poésie de Valéry*, Paris, 1953.
An exhaustive study of the whole of Valéry's poetry.

WEST, J., *Russian Symbolism*, London, 1970.
A study, as the subtitle states, of Vyacheslav Ivanov and the Russian Symbolist aesthetic.

WHITING, C. G., *Valéry, jeune poète*, Paris, 1960.
This volume does for the *Album de Vers Anciens* what Lawler's volume does for *Charmes*, though rather less well.

WILSON, EDMUND, *Axel's Castle, A Study in the Imaginative Literature of 1870–1930*, New York, 1935.
Unlike Symons, Wilson limits himself to 'human symbolism' which he defines as 'an attempt by carefully studied means – a complicated association of ideas represented by a medley of metaphors – to communicate unique personal feelings'. Like

Symons, he begins with a short but lucid introductory essay on Symbolism as he conceives it, and then devotes an essay to each of his chosen authors – who are nearly all different from those chosen by Symons – Yeats, Valéry, Eliot, Proust, Joyce, Stein, Axel (i.e. Villiers de l'Isle Adam) and Rimbaud.

ZIMMERMAN, E., *Magies de Verlaine*, Paris, 1967.
A bigger and more recent study of Verlaine the poet.

Index